PATRIOT HERO

of the Hudson Valley

PATRIOT HERO
of the Hudson Valley

....

The Life & Ride of Sybil Ludington

VINCENT T. DACQUINO

THE
History
PRESS

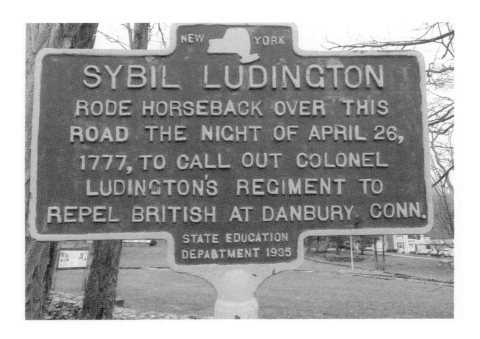

Sybil road marker in Red Mills Park at intersection of 6N and Hill Street in Mahopac Falls, New York.

Published by The History Press
Charleston, SC
www.historypress.com

Cover images, front and back: courtesy Putnam County Historian's Office; *medal*:
Franklin Mint.
All images from the author's collection unless otherwise noted.

First published 2019
Originally Published as *Sybil Ludington: The Call to Arms*
Purple Mountain Press, 2000

Manufactured in the United States

ISBN 9781467140515

Library of Congress Control Number: 2018963667

To my mother, who taught me love
To June, Januarie, Vinny, Christian and Cadence for giving me all the love I need

Sybil Ludington was not only shaped by events in her time, she was also an actor who shaped the events. Some of the history of the Hudson Valley region can be traced in the story of this one individual. Vin Dacquino shows she was a strong woman, a single mother, an entrepreneur whose example of courage and whose accomplishments should be celebrated, in addition to the ride for which she is honored.

—Ron Taylor, president, Patterson Historical Society

CONTENTS

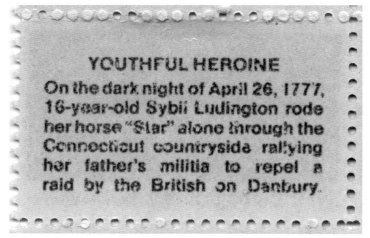

Top: On March 25, 1975, the Daughters of the American Revolution, in collaboration with the United States Postal Service, held a ceremony in Carmel, New York,[1] to celebrate the first-day issue of a stamp that honored Sybil Ludington and proclaimed her a "Contributor to the Cause." Nationwide, seventy-five thousand stamps were sold that day.

Bottom: Note that "on the dark night of April 26, 1777 16-year-old Sybil rode her horse 'Star' alone through the <u>New York</u> countryside rallying her father's militia to repel a raid by British on Danbury, Connecticut."

Acknowledgements

A research project cannot go forward without the cooperation and combined knowledge of many people. It is with heartfelt appreciation that I recognize and thank the following people for their contributions to this project:

J. Banks Smither, commissioning editor, The History Press, for his constant support.

Hilary Parrish, senior editor, The History Press.

Wray Rominger of Purple Mountain Press for believing in Sybil and me enough to publish *Sybil Ludington: The Call to Arms*.

David Hayden for his hard work, patience and editing skills with *Sybil Ludington: The Call to Arms*.

Andrew Campbell, former technical clerk of the Mahopac Public Library, for his continued hard work, strong support and assistance throughout the project.

Ron and Gwen Ludington and the members of the Ludington (Luddington) family for their support.

Kelly Turner and Samuel Abbot, direct descendants of Sybil Ludington, for their correspondence and cooperation.

Paula D. Hunt for her generous time and information in our telephone and e-mail conversations.

Amy Schapiro, technical support staff, Mahopac Library.

Janus Adams, renowned author, editor and advisor.

ACKNOWLEDGEMENTS

Staff of the New-York Historical Society for their assistance with the Ludington Family Papers, in particular Ted O'Reilly, head of the Manuscript Department.

Jane Ross Ludington and Charles Townsend Ludington Jr. for their amazing and generous donation of the Ludington Family Papers.

The members of the weekly writing group at the Mahopac Public Library for their support, comments and suggestions.

Karl Milde, proofreader, critic and supporter.

Mia Brecht, proofreader, critic and supporter.

Tom Jordan, Amy Carlin and the teachers and PTO of Fulmar Road Elementary School for their continued commitment to educating the children of Mahopac about Sybil and her journey.

Stacey Chryssikos and the Arts in Education PNW BOCES for co-sponsoring my lectures and bus tours.

Mariel Carter, adult services reference librarian, Stephenson Public Library, Marinette, Wisconsin.

Kevin White, member of Danbury's Masons Union Lodge 40.

Putnam County historian Sarah Johnson (2014–18), deputy historian Sallie Sypher (1996–present) and aide-to-historian Jennifer Cassidy (2015–present).

Clark Darling, president of Kent Historical Society; Betty Behr, longtime resident of Putnam County; and Kathy Wargas, Elaine Otto, Jacqueline Rohrig Strickland, Jim See, Jim Hoffman and Brian Flood for their support and commitment to local history and Sybil.

Dick Muscarella (1996–2003), Reggie White (2001–16), Katherine Wargas (2000–15) and Christine Mucciolo (1995–2015) of the Putnam County Historian's Office for their help with *The Call to Arms*.

Ron Taylor, president, Patterson Historical Society, for his help with historic facts and the generous use of the 1854 map that includes Ludingtonville.

Karl Rohde, director, Putnam County Veterans' Service Agency.

John Bourges, program coordinator of the PFC Joseph P. Dwyer Vet2Vet Program of Putnam County.

Jim McCarthy, curator, Putnam County Veterans Museum, 2017–18.

Jennifer Pollack, chapter regent (2016–19), Enoch Crosby Chapter, National Society Daughters of the American Revolution.

James Walsh, Eagle Scout, for his work on the Sybil Ludington road signs.

Elizabeth Killian, museum and collections manager, the National Society of the Children of the American Revolution Museum for their generous use of the photo of the Sybil Ludington exhibit.

ACKNOWLEDGEMENTS

George Robinson for his help with notes and bibliography.

Edward Lanyon Woodyard for his contribution of essential information on the Ogden-Connecticut connection.

Everett J. Lee, former historian for the Town of East Fishkill, New York, for his generous gift of four Sybil Ludington stamps and for sharing his personal file on Sybil for *The Call to Arms*.

Raymond Beecher, historian and volunteer librarian at the Greene County Historical Society's Vedder Memorial Research Center in Coxsackie, New York, for the excellent articles by Mabel Parker Smith. Also to Shirley McGrath and staff for their assistance.

Andrew Dancer III, former director of the Catskill Public Library, Catskill, New York, for his help with Sybil's Catskill years.

Wayne Wright at the New York State Historical Association in Cooperstown, New York, for his research assistance.

Tod Butler at the National Archives Research Center in Washington, D.C., for his assistance with the Richard and Edmund Ogden files.

William M. Grace of the Kansas State Historical Society for his aid with information on Edmund Augustus and Fort Riley.

Herbert F. Geller for his interview and the generous gift of his book *A Fight for Liberty*, and Celeste Calvitto of the *Patent Trader* for her assistance in finding Mr. Geller's original articles.

Judy Allen, theater teacher/artist in residence, for sharing a copy of her play *Sibyl's Ride*.

Sharyn Pratt, formerly of the Kent Historical Society, for sharing information on the Ludingtons.

Alan Aimone, military reference specialist; Judith A. Sibley, archives curator; and Sheila Bibes, library technician, of the Special Collections and Archive Division, USMA Library, West Point, New York.

Richard Macello, village historian; Nancy Marcello, village librarian; and William Bauer, town historian, Unadilla, New York.

Staff members of the First Reformed Church of Latter-day Saints, Route 134, Yorktown Heights, New York, for their help in locating Edward Lanyon Woodyard.

Reverend Helen A. Havlik, pastor, the First Presbyterian Church of Unadilla, for her information on early Unadilla.

Barbara Austin and Rod McKenzie of the Fairfield Historical Society for their help with early Ogden genealogy.

Sally Blakelock for her assistance with the records at St. Matthew's Church in Unadilla.

Acknowledgements

Warren and Verna Richards and Gertrude Genung Silbernell, longtime residents of Unadilla, for their discussions of old Unadilla.

Herb Carlson of the Unadilla Masons and the staff at the Chancellor Robert R. Livingston Masonic Library of the Grand Lodge, New York, New York, for their help with Henry Ogden's Masonic years.

Alfred and Lillian Eberhard and the members of the Carmel Historical Society.

Aileen Hayden from the Dutchess Historical Society for her help with Dutchess County research.

Sandra L. Gray, seventh-grade social studies teacher in Newark Valley, New York, for her correspondence and information on textbooks that include mentions of Sybil.

Marion Brophy of Cooperstown for her research at the Otsego County clerk's office.

Pamela LeFever for her generous help with information on the Henry Ogden house and office.

Lincoln Diamant for his generous time and advice.

Nancy Ursprung of Catskill, New York, for sharing information on her home, the site of the former home and tavern of Sybil Ludington.

Barbara Rivette, daughter of Mabel Parker Smith, for sharing her mother's articles on the 1803 epidemic in Catskill.

Opposite: The probable route of Sybil Ludington's night ride through what is now Putnam County, New York.

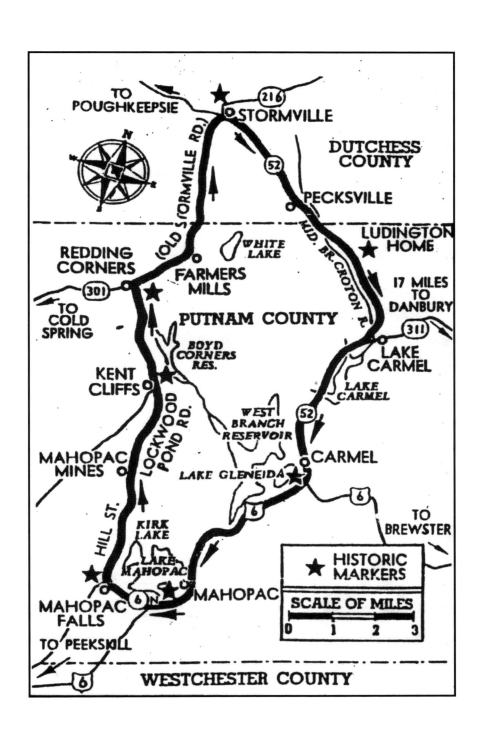

INTRODUCTION

I
t is hard for me to believe that twenty years have passed since I first began my research on Sybil Ludington Ogden. I originally crossed paths with Sybil Ludington one day in 1997 in the small hamlet of Mahopac Falls, forty-five miles north of New York City. I was waiting at a stop sign when I noticed a road marker that read: "Sybil Ludington rode horseback over this road the night of April 26, 1777, to call out Col. Ludington's regiment to repel the British at Danbury, Connecticut." It wasn't the first time I had seen the sign, but it *was* the first I time I actually read it.

As I drove away, it dawned on me that I had been oblivious to an important event of the American Revolution that could have happened in my own neighborhood. I had no idea who Sybil Ludington was when I stopped, but that changed dramatically. My desire to learn more about her became a three-year obsession that took me to Washington, D.C., and through portions of New York State dozens of times. Now, my journey is a twenty-year look back at dozens of speeches, celebrations, bus tours and countless hours of investigating to continue to prove that Sybil Ludington still deserves her place in history for a ride she made on that almost forgotten rainy night in 1777. Perhaps the greatest revelation in my continued research was that my quest to have Sybil known for who she was in the world she lived in is not singular to me. Captivating new articles and books on Sybil continue to be written with new information surfacing annually on an Internet that barely existed when I began my research twenty years ago. A disconcerting fact, however, is that many of the errors

I discovered in literature about Sybil all those years ago continue to be repeated. To set the record straight:

- Sybil was not born in Fredericksburg, New York, where she lived with her family until she was twenty-three.
- She did not marry Henry, Edward or Edmund Ogden.[2]
- Her husband was not a lawyer in Catskill, New York.
- Sybil did not marry her childhood sweetheart.
- She was not the mother of six children: two girls and four boys.
- Her son was not a hero for trying to save women and children in Fort Riley, Kansas.
- Ludingtonville, New York, was not named in honor of her famous ride.
- She did not die at seventy-eight years old.[3]
- She did not ride through Kent, Connecticut, to warn of a British attack.[4]
- The Patriots did not defeat the British in Danbury because of her efforts.[5]
- Sybil was not a "child Patriot" of the Revolutionary War.[6]
- The source for Martha Lamb's information is *not* unknown.
- Her name as it appears on the cover of this book is not the way she herself spelled it.

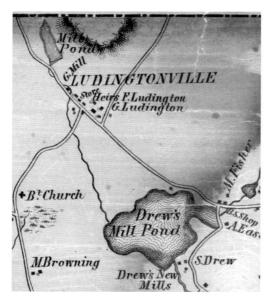

Portion of the 1854 R.F. O'Connor "Map of Putnam County, New York" (id# 002150) from the collection of the Patterson Historical Society. (The small *O*s attached to building symbols designate major outbuildings such as stables or barns.) Note that the map was printed twenty-six years before Sybil's ride was publicly recognized. *Patterson Historical Society.*

THE NAME GAME

The spelling of Sybil's first name has had an interesting history of its own:

In a letter dated April 22, 1854, her nephew called her "Aunt *Sybil*."

Henry Ludington's family register lists Henry's firstborn child as "*Sibyl*, April 5, 1761."[7]

A land deed from Fredericksburg, New York, dated 1793, names "Edmond Ogden and *Sybil* his wife."[8]

In the census of 1810, she is listed as "*Sibel*."

In a letter to her brother Lewis in 1833, Sybil signed the letter "Sister *Sybel* Ogden."

The pension file for Jonathan Carley, 1834, contains a letter from "*Sibel* Ogden."[9]

The pension record application R7777-1838 refers to "*Cybal*," crossed out and changed to "*Sebal*."[10]

In a second letter to her brother one year before her death on January 23, 1838, she signed as "Sister *Sebel* Ogden."

Sybil's gravestone in Patterson, New York, from 1839 reads, "In Memory of *Sibbell* Ludington."[11]

Martha J. Lamb, in her *History of the City of New York*, Vol. 2 in 1880, refers to "his daughter *Sibyl* Ludington."[12]

William Pelletreau, in *History of Putnam County, NY*, 1886, states, "*Sybil* born April 5, 1761."[13]

Howard Louis Conard in *National Magazine* 17 (April 1893) refers to "his daughters *Sibyl* and Rebecca."[14]

Louis S. Patrick in *Connecticut Magazine* (1907) writes, "by his daughters, *Sibbell* and Rebecca."[15]

Willis Fletcher Johnson, in his *Colonel Henry Ludington: A Memoir*, 1907, states, "his daughter *Sibyl*."[16]

The New York State Department of Education road sign from 1935 posts, "*Sibyl* Ludington rode horseback..."

The plaque below Anna Hyatt Huntington's statue, erected in 1961, calls her "*Sybil* Ludington."[17]

A press release from the Bicentennial Celebration Committee in 1977 introduces "*Sybille*."

The roadside grave marker at the Presbyterian church in Patterson cemetery says, "and his daughter *Sybil*."

Most modern-day mentions are of *Sybil* as it appears in this book.

In all these years since her ride, few people, including myself, spell her name the way she did. A signature on a document, signed by Sybil and printed at the top of the document, is clearly spelled "Sebal" Ogden. In another signed document from 1838, Sybil signed as "Sibel."

I began my initial research in 1997, right down the street from my house at the Mahopac Public Library.

"Of course we know of her," Andrew Campbell, a library clerk with a ponytail and glasses, said. "We have a whole vertical file on Sybil Ludington. Have you seen the statue of her down the road here on Lake Gleneida?"

Soon my arms were filled with magazine and newspaper clippings about a girl who made a perilous horseback ride similar to the one made by Paul Revere almost two years earlier, when he rode to rouse the countryside against the British.[18] But there the similarity ends. Revere was a renowned silversmith and a courier for the Massachusetts Assembly carrying messages to the Continental Congress, a man in his forties riding twelve miles of well-traveled country roads near Boston. Sybil was sixteen years old, and her path was an alleged forty miles through dense woods that harbored "Cowboys" and "Skinners." The Cowboys were pro-British marauders who roamed in and around Westchester County plundering farmhouses and stealing cattle they later sold to the British. The Skinners, named for British general Courtland Skinner, had no regular organization. They were separate bands of mounted brigands who claimed attachment sometimes to the British and sometimes to the revolutionaries but were owned by neither. The Skinners did to the Royalists what the Cowboys did to the revolutionaries. Together, they terrorized the countryside as they robbed and killed innocent victims, dragged men off to prisons and molested women.

Henry Wadsworth Longfellow wrote a poem we all read in school about Paul Revere's exploits, but he did not mention that Revere was one of three men who undertook the mission and that he was detained before completing the ride. Sybil made her long journey alone, and she completed her mission.

She received little recognition in her time, yet her story was preserved within her family and passed down through generations. Modern-day critics of Sybil question the authenticity of these family recollections and are often upset by the comparison of Sybil and Revere, a point that will be addressed in a later chapter.

In my early years of research, I believed that the first mention of Sybil's ride was revealed in 1907, 130 years after the event, when details of her ride emerged as part of the family's memoirs in Willis Fletcher Johnson's *Colonel Henry Ludington: A Memoir*. I later discovered that just before the release of

The Presbyterian church in Patterson, Putnam County, New York, where Sybil attended services with her parents and siblings and where she was married in 1784, stood just west of where this present church stands today. Sybil's grave is behind and to the left of this structure built in 1836.

Roadside marker
in front of
the church in
Patterson, New
York.

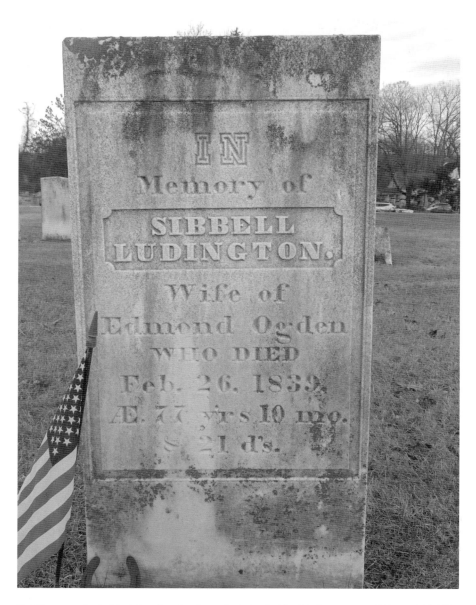

Sybil's grave site behind the church where she is buried beside her parents. Edmond, Sybil's husband, is not buried in Patterson, and though we now know how he died, we do not know what happened to his remains.

One of the many road signs Eagle Scout James Walsh erected along Sybil's route in 2008.

Johnson's memoirs, an article appeared in the *Connecticut Magazine* relating the story of Sybil's ride, "Secret Service of the American Revolution." The article was attributed to Louis S. Patrick (note that his first name here is spelled "Louis") and will be discussed in this book. Both accounts were dated in 1907. This 130-year-old information, passed down from family recollections, plagues her history to this day. Critics pointed out that Willis Fletcher Johnson was hired by members of the Ludington family to write the memoirs on Colonel Ludington. They further pointed out that Lewis S. Patrick was a great-grandson of Colonel Ludington.

Over the next thirty years, the Enoch Crosby Chapter of the Daughters of the American Revolution fought for recognition of Sybil's achievements. The result was the road marker I had seen and others that were placed along her route in 1935. In 2008, new signs, erected by James Walsh, a Mahopac Boy Scout, as part of his Eagle project, were prominently placed to guide residents and tourists along Sybil's approximate route.

Other honors followed the original markers: a bronze equestrian statue of her created by the world-famous sculptor Anna Hyatt Huntington in 1961; an eight-cent United States postage stamp dedicated in her honor in 1975; an opera written by Susan Schefflein and Ludmila Ulehla; countless poems and papers by schoolchildren; and at least two long narrative poems. Most recently, parades and reenactments in both Carmel, New York, and Ridgefield, Connecticut, marked the 240th anniversary of her ride.

Interest in and recognition for Sybil continues to this day, and support and recognition from various individuals, organizations, groups and publishers have fueled my desire to have Sybil Ludington recognized not only statewide but nationally. While I have made steady progress, I have not yet succeeded in having her named as a "National Patriot." *Read Magazine*, in 2005, published my article "A Little Research Goes a Long Way in Solving a History Puzzle," in vol. 54, issue 14 of its national children's magazine.[19] In 2007, *New York State Archives Magazine* published my article "New York Patriot" in its spring issue

Hauntings of the Hudson River Valley, printed in 2008 by The History Press, includes Sybil on the cover and features Sybil in its last chapters.

and even featured Sybil's statue on the front cover of the magazine.[20] In 2017, the article was selected to be included in *The Best of New York Archives: Selections from the Magazine, 2001–2011*.[21] In 2008, two of my books were released: my children's biography, *Sybil Ludington: Discovering the Life of a Revolutionary War Hero*, for young readers, published by Purple Mountain Press,[22] and *Hauntings of the Hudson River Valley: An Investigative Journey*, published by The History Press. The cover of *Hauntings* features Sybil in a haunting pose.[23] On August 1, 2013, I appeared on an episode of the national television program *Monumental Mysteries* in an episode titled "Female Paul Revere" on the season 1, episode 12 program.

Although much of Sybil's biographical information is now being reported correctly, in much of the early published material, errors occurred that threw off researchers for years—mistakes that needed to be rectified. I had no intention of writing a book about Sybil Ludington when I first sought to discover who she was, and I most certainly did not expect to be writing another book about her twenty years later, but I believed when I began the project that a biography about her was imperative to correct the misconceptions I had found. I believe that even more strongly today. Published information about Sybil's life was sparse, often untrue and difficult to locate. Dates often contradicted each other. Simple facts, such as her husband's first name and occupation; where, when and how he died; where she lived after the ride; and even the number of children she had had been incorrect for many years and were repeated without being checked. Some of that misinformation continues to be circulated and repeated even now, almost twenty years after my first book was published.

Letters, public records, articles, books and even letters signed by Sybil have helped me piece together my view of the life of Sybil Ludington, and now, with the advent of the Internet and digital information and the discovery of new family letters and documents, I am able to present even more information.

Sybil herself was my inspiration for my first book and is now the inspiration for this new book. Every attempt has been made to present her accurately with as much information as possible. Both books, developed with the help of many people, are in essence my fight for Sybil's right to be known for who she was in the world in which she lived.

Chapter 1

Before Sybil's Ride

Sybil Ludington was the eldest of the twelve children of Abigail and Henry Ludington. Henry was born in Branford, Connecticut, on May 25, 1739, the son of William and Mary (Knowles) Ludington.[24] Abigail, his first cousin, was born in Southern Dutchess County on May 8, 1745. She was the daughter of Elisha, the tenth child of the Colonel's uncle.[25]

Henry met Abigail when he was on his way to Quebec with Connecticut troops during the French and Indian War. A somewhat romantic account of their meeting was included in Willis Fletcher Johnson's memoir of Colonel Ludington in 1907:

> As the Connecticut troops on their way to that war marched across Dutchess County, New York, through Dover [Plains] and Amenia, it is to be presumed that Henry Ludington on that momentous journey called at his uncle's home, and saw his cousin, afterward to be his wife, who…was at that time consequently a child of about ten years…but we may easily imagine the boy soldier's carrying with him into the northern wilderness an affectionate memory of his little cousin, perhaps the last of his kin to bid him good-by, and also her cherishing a romantic regard for the lad whom she had seen march away with his comrades.[26]

After the Canadian campaign, on May 1, 1760, Henry and Abigail were married. The following April, Sybil was born, and soon afterward, the young family moved to Dutchess County, New York, and settled on 229 acres of undeveloped land in the Philipse Upper Patent. Later, in 1812, their farm became part of the Town of Kent in Putnam County.

When the Ludingtons arrived, they were surrounded by woodlands. The land was fertile and cheap, pasture for the stock abundant and the water good; overall, the place was healthy, pleasant and free from many of the problems of other new settlements, such as Indian raids. With persistence, determination and the cooperation of their growing family, Henry and Abigail worked to make the new land their home. While young Abigail rose to her duties as mother and wife, Henry occupied a position of influence, respect and authority.

Little is known of Abigail's life other than the fact that she bore eleven more children after Sybil. Her courage was crucial to the development of their wilderness life during one of colonial America's most difficult times. Her everyday struggles did not defeat her—she raised twelve children and stood by Henry as he undertook his role as soldier and citizen. Abigail, as is true of many women of her time, received little credit for her dedication to her country, even though her hard work made it possible for her husband to perform his duties well. She lived to be eighty years old in a time when many people died much younger. Abigail died on August 3, 1825. The Colonel died on January 24, 1817, at seventy-eight years old.

Henry was a prominent figure and a subject of interest to historians. "The Colonel," as he was known for most of his life, appears to us in numerous accounts of the times. Above medium height, with blue eyes, he was a husky man with military bearing. As a businessman, he was successful, irreproachable and determined. Despite the demands of his mill, his farm and his family, he was diligent in fulfilling his civic and military duties. He was a member of the New York Assembly from 1777 to 1781 and again in 1786. He was a justice of the peace, town supervisor and overseer of the poor. He also served as sub-sheriff and church trustee for many years and as a member of the Committee of Safety, which was considered the law in many places.

Henry Ludington even purportedly became involved with spies. "John Jay was the acting Judge for this section of Dutchess. Jay and Ludington employed several secret agents to ferret out Tory activities and many prisoners were taken to Judge Jay. Enoch Crosby, who was made famous by James Fenimore Cooper as Harvey Birch in *The Spy*, spent much time at the Ludington home and had a code of secret signals known to Sybil and her sister Rebecca, who were always on guard during their father's absence."[27]

In all, Henry served his community and country for more than sixty years. His military career began when he was seventeen years old, in 1755, when he enlisted in the Second Regiment of Connecticut—troops in the service of the king—and participated in the Battle of Lake George, where he witnessed the horrors of war. His uncle and a cousin were mortally wounded as they fought by his side. He later took part in the French and Indian War from 1756 to 1759. Still, he reenlisted and in 1759 was detailed to escort a company of invalid soldiers from Canada to Boston. The march was made in the dead of winter, and on many nights, with only a blanket for protection, he was forced to dig himself into snowdrifts to avoid freezing. When his rations finally ran out, he ate the bark and twigs of birch trees and berries that he scavenged from the frozen countryside. Nonetheless, he survived to complete his mission.[28]

Soon after Henry arrived in Dutchess County in 1761, he became sub-sheriff and swore an oath to remain faithful to the king, "to defend Him against all traitorous conspiracies and attempts against his person, crown and dignity to the utmost of his power, and particularly to uphold the succession of the crown against the claims of the pretended Prince of Wales, who had styled himself King of England under the name of James the Third."[29]

William Tryon, the captain-general and governor of the Province of New York, appointed Henry captain of the Fifth Company of the Second Battalion of the Fredericksburgh Regiment of Militia in Dutchess County. On February 13, 1773, Henry accepted a commission as captain in Colonel Beverly Robinson's Dutchess County regiment. Soon after, his loyalty to the king dwindled, and he resigned his commission in favor of the revolutionary cause.

It was a period in American history when enemies could live next door or hide waiting and armed behind trees or near an outhouse. Real battles with loss of life occurred in taverns and in skirmishes in backyards between revolutionaries and their Royalist neighbors and former friends. Family arguments began in one-room schoolhouses and in April planting fields, where men tended the land, ready in an instant to respond to the call for battle in defense of their families.

Henry's military experience influenced the Patriots' Provincial Congress of the Colony of New York to appoint him to the rank of colonel in the summer of 1776. A new provincial congress, calling itself the Convention of the Representatives of the State of New York, also commissioned Henry as a colonel. His regiment, the Seventh of the Dutchess County militia, was thereafter referred to as Colonel Ludington's regiment.

Colonel Ludington's area of command in Dutchess County was along the most direct route the British might take to and from Connecticut and the coast on Long Island Sound. He was forced to bring his regiment into "active and constant service in the counties of Dutchess and Westchester, either to assist the regular troops, or to quell the turbulent Tory spirit of that section, or to repress the vicious and exasperating conduct of the 'Cowboys and Skinners.'"[30]

One record described the Colonel's section as "deplorable."

> *Small parties of volunteers on one side, and parties of Royalists and Tories on the other, constantly harassed the inhabitants and plundered without mercy friend and foe alike. To guard against surprise required the utmost vigilance. Within this territory resided many friends of the American cause, whose situation exposed them to continual ravages by Tories, horse thieves, and cowboys, who robbed them indiscriminately and mercilessly, while personal abuse and punishment were almost incredible.*[31]

Colonel Ludington and his regiment often prevented marauders from obtaining supplies for the British forces. Much of General Howe's cattle and grain came from Cowboys and thieves. The Colonel's success enraged Howe, who put a price on Colonel Ludington's head of 300 English guineas, "dead or alive!"[32] In his 1854 letter regarding his grandfather (Colonel Ludington), Charles H. Ludington quoted the reward as "several hundred pounds."

Henry was also deeply involved in his family life and in the workings of his farm and gristmill. Erected in 1776, the gristmill was the first in his neighborhood. It enjoyed a fine reputation for quality milling and had the distinction of being built almost solely by women because most of the men were away in military service.[33]

Henry and Abigail raised twelve children in the Ludington house. Their births were recorded in the Colonel's family register and inscribed on the flyleaf of one of the ledgers he used in his many capacities as a public servant:[34]

Sibyl, April 5, 1761.
Rebecca, January 24, 1763.
Mary, July 31, 1765.
Archibald, July 5, 1767.
Henry, March 28, 1769.
Derick, February 17, 1771.

Tertullus, Monday Night, April 19, 1773.
Abigail, Monday Morning, February 26, 1776.
Anna, at sunset, March 14, 1778.
Frederick, June 10, 1782.
Sophia, May 16, 1784.
Lewis, June 25, 1786.

Note: A copy of this ledger also appears in a letter from Charles H. Ludington to William Pelletreau dated January 16, 1786, in Box 1 File #2, "Ludington Family Papers, 1776–1945," MS 2962. Also note that written next to Sybil's name is "Henry Ogden."

On the surface, Sybil's life was free from many of the hardships of the time. Her parents were far from poor, and her father had great influence in the county. However, she bore many burdens on her young shoulders. The eldest of twelve children, she was expected to take a prominent role in raising her siblings. In addition, she had to face the reality that her father might leave home some morning and never return or that a shot could ring out at any time and take him as he sat at the family table. Sybil's world of "simple country-girl prosperity" was actually a complex maze of uncertainty, fear and bravery. Given the turmoil of the times, Sybil was compelled to take a leading role in protecting her father, who was a wanted man. An incident reported by Charles H. Ludington in 1854, later recounted by Martha J. Lamb in 1880 and again by Lewis S. Patrick in 1907, illustrated the extent of her commitment toward this end.

One night, Ichobod Prosser, a notorious Tory, came with hopes of getting the large reward posted on the Colonel's head. Prosser's men surrounded the house and prepared to attack, but Sybil, her mother, her sister Rebecca and younger siblings outsmarted them:

> *These fearless girls, with guns in hand were acting as sentinels, pacing the piazza to and fro in true military style and grit to guard their father against surprise and to give him warning of any approaching danger. They discovered Prosser and his men and gave the alarm. In a flash, candles were lighted in every room of the house and the few occupants marched and counter-marched before the windows and from this simple and clever ruse, Prosser was led to believe that the house was strongly guarded and did not dare to make an attack. He kept his men concealed behind the trees and fences until day break, when with yells they resumed their march and hastened southwards toward New York City, ignorant of how they had been*

THE LUDINGTON HOME

Over the years, the Ludington home became known far and wide for showing good cheer to travelers. Guests received the warmest hospitality. The Ludingtons entertained General Washington; General Rochambeau; and William Ellery of Massachusetts, a signer of the Declaration of Independence, among many others. The Colonel, in his later years, is said to have lived there entertaining and sitting with friends such as John Jay, smoking his pipe and exchanging stories about the days of the Revolution.[35]

The Ludington house has been described as built prior to the Revolution and in a style similar to almost every house of the period: two stories in the front and one in the rear. Huge doors divided in the middle with ponderous latches gave entrance. A piazza with large and spacious rooms, their ceilings low and the floors nicely sanded, ornamented the front. Wide halls divided the rooms, and a massive stairway led up to commodious chambers. Immense chimneys rose within the structures, each with a wide fireplace and large oven.[36]

Another source states the house was several times enlarged. The main building was two stories in height, with an attic above. Through the center ran a broad hall, with a stairway broken with a landing and turn. At one side was a parlor and at the other a sitting or living room, and back of each of these was a bedroom. The parlor was wainscoted and ceilinged with planks of the fragrant and beautiful red cedar. Beyond the sitting room, at the side of this main building, was the "weaving room," an apartment unknown to our domestic economy but essential in colonial days. It was a large room fitted with a handloom, a number of spinning wheels, reels, swifts and other paraphernalia for the manufacture of homespun fabrics of different kinds. This room also

The Ludington Mill consisted of a post-and-girt frame, fastened with wooden pegs and hand-wrought square nails. The building was twenty-four by thirty-six feet and was two and a half stories high. It was built in 1776 and destroyed by a fire in 1972, just months before it was to be restored by the Putnam Historical Society. *Courtesy Putnam County Historian's Office.*

A bearded Vin Dacquino lectures students at the Ludington Mill foundation in 2011. Members of the Kent Historical Society continue to work today to restore the Ludington Mill and build a museum to honor Sybil and her father.

contained a huge stone fireplace. Beyond it, at the extreme east of the house, was the kitchen, with its great fireplace and brick or stone oven. The house fronted toward the south and commanded a fine outlook over one of the picturesque landscapes for which that region is famed.[37]

In 1838, seventy-six years after the Ludingtons moved to Dutchess County and one year before Sybil died, the Ludington house was torn down.

foiled by clever girls. The Colonel's most vigilant and watchful companion was his sentinel daughter, Sibbell. Her constant care and thoughtfulness, combined with fortuitous circumstances, prevented the fruition of many an intrigue against his life and capture.[38]

The first public mention of this daring act appeared in Martha Lamb's book. Although not surprisingly similar, it did offer details not in Patrick's description and vice versa:

His [the Colonel's] *house was surrounded one night by a band of Tories from Quaker Hill, while on their route to join the British in New York and but for the presence of mind and spirit of his two young daughters, Sibyl and Rebecca, he would undoubtedly have been taken. These fair maidens were keeping watch as sentinels with guns in their hands on the piazza. They discovered the approach of the foe in time to cause candles lighted in every room, and the few occupants of the house passed and repassed the windows continually. The ruse led the assaulting party to believe the house was strongly guarded, and, hiding behind the trees and fences, watched until daybreak for signs of repose. Ere it was light enough to discover by whom they had been held in check, they vented their disappointment in unearthly yells and rapidly fled.*[39]

Patrick's and Johnson's accounts were in 1907. Lamb's account was in 1880. Patrick gave a name to the Tory that Lamb omitted. Did Patrick have documentation for the event that Lamb didn't possess? Perhaps an eyewitness account or a family letter? Who could have offered her such details of an event that happened about two generations earlier? Apparently, it was someone who knew more of the early Sybil than the later-day Sybil. In her footnote, Lamb cites one of the Colonel's "well-known grandchildren" as "Major Edward A. Ogden of the United States army (who died at Fort Riley, Kansas, in 1855) son of Sibyl Ludington, who married the Hon. Edward Ogden." Actually, Brevet Major *Edmund* A. Ogden was *Sybil's* grandson and the Colonel's *great*-grandson, and she married *Edmond* Ogden, who was not necessarily entitled to be called "Honorable." (Remember that some early accounts claimed Edmond to be an attorney.)[40]

Could Lamb's source have been Lewis S. Patrick or some other family member? Did she reveal his news about Sybil's ride twenty-seven years before he did? Patrick was already about thirty-seven when Lamb published her book in 1880. Patrick was the son of Caroline Ludington Patrick, who was the daughter of Frederick Ludington, Sybil's younger brother. Willis Fletcher Johnson, author of *Colonel Henry Ludington: A Memoir*, tells us in his preface that "the most copious and important data have been secured from the manuscript collections of two of Henry Ludington's descendants, Mr. Lewis S. Patrick of Marinette, Wisconsin [grandson of Sybil's brother Frederick], who has devoted much time and painstaking effort to the work of searching for and securing authentic information on his distinguished ancestor [Colonel Henry Ludington] and Mr. Charles Ludington, of New York [son of Sybil's brother Lewis], who has received many valuable papers and original documents from a descendant of Sybil Ludington Ogden, Henry Ludington's first-born child."

After an exhausting and sometimes frustrating search for the records of Lewis S. Patrick in New York, Wisconsin, Michigan and Washington, D.C., I came to the conclusion that his research, the research that was used by Martha J. Lamb and Willis Fletcher Johnson, was at least in part missing, and perhaps some of it is, but it was not the only research material used to tell Sybil's and the Colonel's stories.

At the end of the memoir, in a chapter titled "After the War," Johnson tells about

a letter written in April 1881 to Mr. Patrick by Mrs. Julia L. Comfort, of Catskill, New York, a daughter of Colonel Ludington's son, Tertullus Ludington.

Speaking of the old homestead at Frederickstown, and the family there, she writes in a letter, quoted completely on pages 213 and 214 of the Memoirs:

"I was so young when last there, and consequently do not remember much about them. It was the winter before Grandma Luddington died. She gave my Mother Grandfather's gun and sword, and I think the powder horn to my brother Henry because he was named after him. They were all mounted in silver. The first time we were there was in the fall when chestnuts were ripe." *She talks about cutting down the tree and then mentions the Colonel and her father, Tertullus. "My father was with us, and Grandfather said to him, (he always called him Tarty,) 'I am going to make a will, and I owe you for five barrels of pork, but as I have not got the money just now I will remember it in my will.'"* *After continuing the details of the agreement, Mrs. Comfort mentions Sybil in the last paragraph of the letter.*

"The last time Aunt Ogden was there, she was telling us about how she and Aunt Sophia (probably a slip of the pen for Rebecca) were alone in the house in war time (Revolutionary War). They had had a fence built around the house and they each had a gun, and once in awhile they would fire one off to make the soldiers think there were men in the house."[41]

July 10, 2018

On July 10, 2018, I took my third trip to the New-York Historical Society Museum and Library, and the result was breathtaking. In a file marked "Ludington Family Papers, 1776–1945," I found the mother lode of Sybil Ludington information donated in 2015 by Mrs. Jane Ludington, prepared with annotated notes by Charles Henry Ludington, grandson of Colonel Ludington, that had apparently gone unnoticed by researchers. Jane's husband, Charles Townsend Ludington Jr., is Charles's grand descendant. In addition to a six-page account of the life of the Colonel and his daughter, handwritten to "Martha Lamb" and dated 1778, two years before her published article on the Ludingtons in *History of the City of New York*, there was another twenty-one-page sketch dated 1879 and several boxes of family correspondence and memorabilia. The collection included a faded letter to Henry Deming, Esq., dated April 22, 1854, regarding Sybil's ride and daring attempt to save her father from capture. Although some of the letter was too difficult to read, the following was quite legible:

to Henry Deming Esquire   April 22, 1854

Dear Sir

    Mrs. W.H. Clark of Danbury has informed me this day that you are to deliver an oration on Thursday next, April 27th in the completion of the monument to General Wooster. I am very sorry that I had not known of this before for I could have had access to some records in Putnam County in this State and could have put you in possession of many interesting incidents. At present, my business will prevent my leaving New York. I should be glad to be in Danbury on the 27th.

    I have been grieved at the neglect and injustice done to the memory of my Grandfather Col. Henry Ludington who bore an important part in the engagement which succeeded the burning of Danbury. He held his commission from Washington and his regiment was made up of the hardy militia of the town of Kent in the then County of Dutchess and vicinity and he was a terror to the Tories and Cowboys who infested that district.

    On the evening of the 25th of April 1777, a messenger arrived at his home with the intelligence that the British under Gen. Tryon had landed at Old Well and were marching toward Danbury. After dressing himself, he put my Aunt Sybil, a young girl of about fourteen [age unclear] on horseback in the dead of night dispatched her to Cold Spring a distance of some 25 miles through a country infested with Cowboys and Skinners to inform Gen'l Putnam who was stationed there. He then sounded the alarm and by daybreak his regiment was on the march toward Danbury.

    In conjunction with Genl Wooster he did reach to harass the enemy in their retreat after the destruction of the village. His men who were excellent marksmen picked off many of the British. A barricade was made just above Ridgefield where Gen'l Wooster was surrounded. All along the route of the retreating enemy, obstructions were placed in the roads and an incessant fire kept up at times from every convenient place. Gen'l Wooster had too few troops to attack the enemy openly with much chance of success. At Old Well my grandfather's regiment opened fire on them while embarking and after they had started for their vessels.

    Colonel Ludington held a commission in the late French War and served with credit in Canada. He was an aid to Washington at the battle of White Plains and was much complimented by the Gen'l in his soldiering bravery and the fine appearance of his regiment. He was an intimate friend and confidant of Enoch Crosby the spy who he often let into his home in the dead of night when abroad in some of his dangerous expeditions. Colonel Howe offered a reward of several hundred pounds for his capture and declared him a [illegible] and dangerous traitor. Several unsuccessful attempts were made to affect this. About fifty Tories whose [illegible] in Quaker Hill surrounded his home one night while on their march to join the British at New York. A friend in the company managed to apprise of this danger.

He was entirely unprotected but his wife and two daughters being with him, but they cunningly deceived the enemy by placing lights in the different rooms and by quickly moving from one part to another as though [the rest mostly faded and indistinguishable]....

Truly
Charles H. Ludington

On the day after my discovery, I made a quick call to Brigid Gurtin, executive director of the Danbury Museum and Historical Society, to confirm the names and events in the letter. She informed me that it was all there on page 424 in James Montgomery Bailey's *History of Danbury, Conn., 1684–1896*. A celebration for the completion of the Wooster monument was indeed held on April 27, 1854, hosted by the Danbury Masons. Brother Henry C. Deming delivered the oration, and David Clark was the grand master.[42]

The letter was written by Charles Henry Ludington, son of Sybil's brother Lewis Ludington. Twenty-four years later, however, Charles gave Martha J. Lamb a slightly different account of Sybil's ride, omitting information about the twenty-five-mile trip to Cold Spring to apprise General Putnam of Tryon's attack. In a six-page letter transcribed in his own handwriting with a note stating, "Sent to Mrs. Lamb" and dated "Jany 1878" (See Box 1 in File 2 MS 2962 at the New-York Historical Society Research Center for a copy of the letter), he wrote:

When troops were sent under Gen'l Tryon to burn the stores at Danbury Conn. a messenger arrived at Colonel Ludington's on Saturday Evening April 26th 1777. His men were scattered at their homes at a distance of many miles and no one could be found to summon them together until his young daughter Sybil a girl of sixteen mounted her horse with a man's saddle and in the dead of night volunteered to do this service. By breakfast-time the next morning the regiment was on its way to Danbury.

Note here that Charles in 1854 states Sybil "mounted her horse with a man's saddle." A letter written by Sybil's niece in 1894 states, "Aunt Sybil mounted a horse at a moment's warning and with only a halter to guide him, no saddle or even a bridle." The statue by Anna Hyatt Huntington in 1961 has her riding sidesaddle.

The files in MS 2962 contained a great deal of correspondence from Ludington relatives, including a letter in 1894 from Laura Ann Ludington

Hustis, Charles Henry's sister, who recounted the stories told by her Aunt Sybil and Aunt Rebecca. The letter included information about Sybil's ride, protecting her father and her possible presence at Fort Montgomery when it was taken by the British in October 1777. It also said that the likely first meeting place of Sybil and her husband-to-be, Edmund Ogden, might have been at "Washington's inauguration," which is unlikely since she married Edmund in 1783; the inauguration was in 1789.

I was unable to find a letter written of the event explaining why Charles Henry later omitted General Putnam from his account of the ride, and I could find no mention of a letter from a niece to "Mr. Patrick," which was included on page 213 and 214 in Willis Fletcher Johnson's memoirs of Colonel Henry.

Chapter 2

SYBIL'S RIDE

S o, let us examine the more recognized version of Sybil's famous ride and the events leading up to it. In April 1777, a chain of events began that challenged Sybil's courage—the British march on Danbury, Connecticut, and the subsequent burning of that city.

The commissioners of the Continental army had been using Danbury as a depot for military stores, and British general William Tryon was assigned to prevent their use by enemies of the king. On April 24, 1777, twenty transports and six war vessels left New York Harbor for Compo Beach in Connecticut. Troops reached Compo the next day and debarked, ready to begin the long march to Danbury. Tryon's men proceeded as if on parade. One soldier was described in detail:

> *Upon his head a metallic cap, sword-proof, surmounted by a cone, from which a long, chestnut-colored plume fell to his shoulders. Upon the front of the cap was a death's head, under which was inscribed the words: "Or Glory." A red coat faced with white, an epaulette on each shoulder, buckskin breeches of a bright yellow, black knee boots, and spurs completing the costume. A long sword swung at his side, and a carbine was carried, muzzle down, in a socket at his stirrup. These were models of discipline and military splendor, and mounted on handsome chargers, sixteen hands high.*[43]

Another detachment, the Sixty-Fourth Foot—a grenadier regiment—wore "high grenadier caps and red coats faced with black." This "parade" of the king's forces marched steadily through Connecticut toward an unsuspecting Danbury.

Word spread ahead of the British, and Connecticut revolutionaries mustered to resist as best they could along the route of the march. Generals David Wooster and Benedict Arnold, receiving intelligence at New Haven, gathered a small escort and pushed westward, picking up various militia companies as they advanced. Meanwhile, General Gold Selleck Silliman with five hundred militiamen was already on the trail of Tryon. Colonel Henry Ludington came in from New York with four hundred reinforcements. This number has been contested recently in Stephen Darley's *Call to Arms: The Patriot Militia in the 1777 British Raid on Danbury*.

One Connecticut regiment, known as the "Gallant Seventeen," hid in the shadows of the moonlit night waiting to ambush the advancing column. They struck out of the darkness, killing a number of soldiers, with only one American slightly wounded, but they did not stop the march. The British loaded their dead and wounded in an oxcart, sent them back to the ships and continued on. After passing what is now called Aspetuck, the Royalist troops stopped in the parish of Weston, where they probably rested.

Rumors spread like wildfire among the threatened citizens. One story that reached Redding held that General Tryon was out to kill young boys because they would grow into soldiers. "The women of Redding had heard of this propensity and at his approach gathered all the boys of thirteen and under… and conveyed them to a secluded place near[by] where they were left under the charge of one Gershom Barlow. Here they remained until the invader had regained his ships, provisions being cooked and sent to them daily."[44]

One Redding mother, Rebecca Sanford Barlow, earned a place in history because she stayed with her sick children to face the enemy while most of her neighbors fled in fear. "The terrified inhabitants resolved on instant flight. Each family gathered together such of their effects as they could take with them and quickly quit the village, traveling the whole night to reach a place of refuge. Mrs. Barlow had two sick children and could not carry them away. To leave them was out of the question, so she and her family remained alone to face the enemy, deserted by all her neighbors."[45] Some hid in barns and forests; others escaped the area with all the goods they could gather in carts and wagons. Parents had to face the horrifying decision to accompany their families to safety or stay and do what they could to secure their homes against the enemy.

In a place called Couch's Rock in Weston, Connecticut, a small regiment of revolutionaries under Captain Zalmon Read met with British troops in full force and was immediately taken captive with no fatalities, sending a clear message that this was an enemy to be reckoned with. From there, the British troops moved across the Weston border into Redding and proceeded through the town causing no destruction or casualties. At Redding's Ridge, they stopped for breakfast and relaxed in the comfort of Royalist hospitality. At the time, Redding was known as "Tory country." Although no buildings were destroyed, several prisoners were taken.

Before reaching Danbury, the two-thousand-man British force had to pass through Bethel, Connecticut. Rain fell heavily throughout the night, causing difficult conditions for soldiers on both sides. A man named Luther Holcomb put the British army on edge by marching to the top of a hill pretending to be followed by a number of troops. "Halt the whole universe! Wheel into kingdoms and prepare to attack!" he shouted. The British believed him enough to prepare for battle, but when it was realized that there would be no attack, they marched quietly out of Bethel in the rain without incident. As they left, American troops slipped in quietly behind them at 11:30 p.m. under the direction of Generals Benedict Arnold, David Wooster and Gold Selleck Silliman. Together, they ordered six hundred men to prepare to fight the British in the pouring rain with muskets that could barely shoot in dry weather. They waited in Bethel for the return of the British, hoping for a surprise attack, but Tryon brought his troops back through Ridgefield after his night in Danbury.

On the following afternoon, the enemy reached Danbury in sunshine between two and three o'clock, but another storm was on its way, bringing the additional heavy rains that Sybil would be forced to ride through that night. As the afternoon continued, a few incidents occurred. British soldiers chased one horseman through the streets. He escaped when he unrolled a bolt of cloth he was carrying and frightened a pursuer's horse. A second incident involved four young men who shot into a column of soldiers from the house of Captain Ezra Starr, which was raided immediately after the shots rang out. The house was burned along with the bodies of the men who had been accused of the shooting.

As the day proceeded, British soldiers continued to take control of Danbury. "As the British troops reached a point near the present location of the court-house their artillery was discharged and the heavy balls, six and twelve-pounders, flew screaming up the street, carrying terror to the hearts of the women and children, and dismay to the heads of the homes thus endangered."[46]

John Porter came into the village to see what was happening. Porter was "a man of powerful build, with muscles like steel, and a movement that was a very good substitute for lightning." When he was told to halt, he stood tall against them and asked, "What for?" He advanced on them, and they said, "You are our prisoner." He continued his move on them. "Guess not," he said. They were close upon him, but there was a gully behind them. In a flash, he had the foremost trooper in his grasp. In the next instant, he hurled him against the other two, and the three of them tumbled into the gully in a demoralized heap. The rest of the squad, seeing the disaster, immediately surrounded and subdued Porter. Porter and a man named Barnum are believed to be the only prisoners the enemy carried away from Danbury. They were thrown into a New York prison called Sugar House Prison. Porter was released eventually, but Barnum later died there of starvation.[47]

British troops remained in Danbury all day destroying Patriot military stores. Those goods found in a Church of England and goods found in the homes of Royalists were taken into the street to be burned and their buildings spared, but houses owned by revolutionaries and used as storehouses for grain and meat were burned to the ground. "It is said that the fat from the burning meat ran ankle-deep in the street. No less free ran the rum and wine, although not in the same direction!"[48]

As night began, drunken brawls and loud laughter became more frequent. "The drunken men went up and down Main Street in squads, singing army songs, shouting coarse speeches, hugging each other, swearing, yelling, and otherwise conducting themselves as becomes an invader when he is very, very drunk."[49]

During some of the day and most of the night, Connecticut farmers sneaked back into the enemy camp to kill an occasional soldier. All around them, revolutionary troops were being mustered until, finally, General Tryon gave an order to move out.

By midnight, three Danbury buildings had been burned and many of the drunken revelers were sleeping soundly. By about one o'clock Sunday morning, Tryon ordered the gathering of soldiers, and the work of real destruction began. More buildings were burned. Those owned by Tories were marked with a cross, which protected them; houses without crosses were torched.

In the meantime, as the flames filled a rainy night sky, dispatchers rode frantically in all directions, and American troops rallied to a belated defense of Danbury.

LEWIS S. PATRICK

Lewis S. Patrick is acknowledged on page 219 of the Ludington memoirs as a "great-grandson of Colonel Henry Ludington, through his son Frederick, husband of Susanna Griffith, and the latter's daughter Caroline wife of Rowland Patrick." Johnson credits Patrick as follows: "To his painstaking and untiring labors must be credited the collection of a large share of the data used upon which this memoir of his ancestor is founded."[50] Note that the Johnson spelling of "Lewis" does not agree with the spelling of "Louis" in an article in the *Connecticut Magazine*, but it is likely they are one and the same person. Much of the information in the 1907 article is nearly identical to information in the memoirs. "Louis" S. Patrick was a respected historian. In his *Connecticut Magazine* article, he was referred to as one "who has made an extended study of this phase of the American Revolution." It is this article that was first thought to have revealed Sybil's story to the public. Note also that he signed an application for the Sons of the American Revolution as "Lewis S. Patrick."[51]

In his later years, Lewis Patrick served as personal secretary to Senator Isaac Stephenson of Wisconsin. His duties ended with a sudden heart attack on a street in Washington, D.C., on July 2, 1913. His complete files used by Willis Fletcher Johnson for *Colonel Henry Ludington: A Memoir* are yet to be found. Several letters and correspondence to Charles H. Ludington and Lewis Ludington can be found in the box in the New-York Historical Society research room as part of the "Ludington Family Papers, 1776–1945" MS 2962.

Before long, a rider roused the Ludington household, and Sybil was galloping into the night on her way to muster the Colonel's regiment. W.F. Johnson told the story of her ride in 1907. It was presumed that he based his information on the records of Lewis S. Patrick, the Colonel's great-grandson.[52] Note that the location of her ride correlates with the 1854 letter of Charles Ludington to Henry Deming ("Carmel to Coldspring").

According to Johnson:

> *At eight or nine o'clock that evening a jaded horseman reached Colonel Ludington's home with the news. We may imagine the fire that flashed through the veteran's veins at the report of the dastardly act of his former chief.* [General Tryon, the last of the British governors of

New York, had appointed Colonel Ludington a captain in a colonial regiment before the Colonel became a revolutionary.] *But what to do? His regiment was disbanded; its members scattered at their homes, many at considerable distances.* [It was April, planting season, and the farmers needed to tend their fields and had been granted leaves to get their farm work done.] *He must stay there to muster all who came in. The messenger from Danbury could ride no more, and there was no neighbor within call. In this emergency he turned to his daughter Sybil, who, a few days before,* [actually three weeks] *had passed her sixteenth birthday, and bade her to take a horse, ride for the men, and tell them to be at his house by daybreak. One who even rides now from Carmel to Cold Spring will find rugged and dangerous roads, with lonely stretches. Imagination only can picture what it was a quarter and a century ago* [now over two centuries ago] *on a dark night, with reckless bands of "Cowboys" and "Skinners" abroad in the land. But the child performed her task, clinging to a man's saddle, and guiding her steed with only a hempen halter, as she rode through the night bearing the news of the sack of Danbury. There is no extravagance in comparing her ride with that of Paul Revere and its midnight message. Nor was her errand less efficient than his was. By daybreak, thanks to her daring, nearly the whole regiment was mustered before her father's house at Fredricksburgh, and an hour or two later was on the march for vengeance on the raiders.*[53]

Where did Sybil ride? Today, it is believed she rode through Carmel, Mahopac, Mahopac Mines and eventually to Stormville and back to what is today called Ludingtonville. There are signs along her route to mark the way, as mentioned earlier in this book. I even presented a probable map of it on page 10 of my first book about her ride, *Sybil Ludington: The Call to Arms.* We must also note that Charles Ludington quoted the distance from Sybil's house to Cold Spring as about twenty-five miles, making her round trip approximately fifty miles through a country infested with Cowboys and Skinners. So, when and how did Sybil's ride change from a ride to Cold Spring to a ride south to Shaw's Pond, now Lake Gleneida at Carmel, then on to Lake Mahopac to Mahopac Falls and eventually Stormville and home? The answer comes in an article written by Raymond H. Torrey, secretary of the American Scenic and Historic Preservation Society, published in the *New York Herald Tribune* on Sunday, September 9, 1934. The article, titled "Signs to Mark Historic Ride of Revolutionary Heroine to Be Seen by Motorists Tomorrow," details a program of the Board of Regents of the University of the State of New York created in observance of the 150th anniversaries of the events of the American Revolution. The State Education Department, under the direction of Alexander C. Flick, state historian, promoted investigations into unmarked historical sites by organizations and individuals interested in aiding the department. The result was hundreds of blue and gold cast-iron markers placed along well-traveled highways in New York State, such as the one I had seen near my home. Through historic investigations to identify local heroes and places, including Putnam County, Enoch Crosby, Henry Ludington and Sybil Ludington, with the cooperation of prominent members of the Enoch Crosby Chapter of the Daughters of the American Revolution; George Turner, a descendant of Colonel Ludington through marriage; Chester D. Pugsley, a trustee of the American Scenic and Preservation Society; and the writer of the article, Raymond H. Torrey, "a probable route of Sibyl's ride" was established. The route was carefully mapped out using the addresses of officers in Colonel Ludington's regiment who would alert key people in each vicinity to alert more militia. The article continued with a detailed description of the ride using a 1778 map created by Robert Erskine, surveyor general of the American army. Irving S. Adler, assistant to Dr. Flick, cordially approved the idea of marking Sybil's route with at least a dozen markers. Many of those markers still exist today.

In his dramatic rendition of Sybil's ride, Johnson is not correct when he refers to Sybil as a "child." Sybil's world wasn't the world we live in today. Sybil's mother, Abigail, for example, was only fourteen when she married Henry. Sybil was a very capable young woman at sixteen and was engaged in the revolutionary cause beyond just helping to protect her father or doing domestic chores. The story of her conspiring with Enoch Crosby, a notorious spy, attests to this fact, although, as is the case with much of Sybil's history, there was no written documentation to back this up. Today, we have the letter from Charles H. Ludington mentioned earlier and letters from other family members to support the claims, and as for her courageous ride, whether it was through "what is now Putnam county to Cold Spring to alert General Putnam who was stationed near there," as Charles Ludington stated in his earlier version of her ride, or through what is now Putnam County to alert her father's troops closer to her home, it was a daring risk of her life. Sybil knew the roads and where the men lived, perhaps as a result of riding with her father along the narrow dirt roads of Mahopac and Carmel. They

Sybil mustered her father's men here at the parade ground on April 27, 1777.

undoubtedly laid out the best route to be used to muster the regiment in times of emergency. It is doubtful that she had to rouse each of the four hundred men individually or that every one of the Colonel's men mustered to the call. It is more likely that she rode to her father's officers as an appeal for them to arouse their own men. Key people in each village undoubtedly heard her banging on their shutters and, in turn, alerted the local contingent while she rode on to complete her mission. In the morning, Colonel Ludington's regiment was gathered in a place on his property known as the "parade grounds," preparing to face the enemy. Today, two gas stations occupy what was once the training grounds, but a road sign marks the spot.

During the night, Tryon was forced to make decisions. Earlier hopes to take captured supplies to New York City for British use were abandoned. Additional supplies would slow him down and make it impossible to fight those on their way to engage him. He chose instead to burn as much of the stores as possible to prevent their use by the revolutionaries. The next morning, Sunday, April 27, it was clear to General Tryon that he would have to make it back to Compo by way of Ridgefield and get his men aboard the ships as quickly as possible to avoid the troops at Bethel.[54] General Alexander McDougall was marching in from Peekskill, and Colonel Ludington was on his way from Dutchess County. By this time, however, the troops from Bethel had crossed over into Ridgefield. McDougall had 1,200 men to support the 600 to 800 from Bethel. Behind them were the troops from Dutchess County, consisting of another possible 400 men. Johnson described them this way:

> *They were a motley company, some without arms, some half-dressed, but all filled with a certain berserk rage. That night they reached Ridgefield and*

joined Arnold, Wooster, and Silliman. The next morning they encountered the British at Ridgefield. They were short of ammunition and were outnumbered by the British three to one. But they practiced the same tactics that Paul Revere's levies at Lexington and Concord found so effective. Their scattering sharpshooter fire from behind trees and fences and stone walls, harassed the British sorely, and made their retreat to their ships at Compo resemble a rout. Nor were instances of individual heroism in conflict lacking. Arnold had his horse shot from under him as, almost alone, he furiously charged the enemy, and the gallant Wooster received a wound from which he died a few days later. There were far greater operations in the war than this, but there was scarcely one more expeditious, intrepid and successful. Writing of it to Gouverneur Morris, Alexander Hamilton said, "I congratulate you on the Danbury expedition. The stores destroyed there have been purchased at a high price to the enemy. The spirit of the people on the occasion does them great honor—is a pleasing proof that they began the contest and will be a galling discouragement to the enemy from repeating attempts of the kind. The people of New York considered the affair in the light of a defeat to the troops."[55]

The British never again dared to attack the Connecticut interior.

Tryon reached Ridgefield more slowly than he had expected and, after burning a mill belonging to Isaac Keeler, stopped his troops for lunch and rest just outside North Salem. At that point, General Wooster attacked Tryon but was counterattacked. Wooster retreated but returned. On his return and attack of the rear guard, he was fatally wounded.

A small plaque hangs adjacent to present-day Route 116 in Ridgefield to mark the spot where General David Wooster was shot. An engraved sign was placed on what is now a busy thoroughfare.

GENERAL DAVID WOOSTER

An excerpt from his obituary published in *Historical Collections of Connecticut* reads:

The British had six pieces of artillery, three in the front and three guarding the rear. The screaming of the grape-shot and the whistling of the balls frightened the militiamen and they hesitated in charging. Wooster endeavored to rally them and turning in his saddle shouted, "Come on, my boys, never mind such random shots!" While leading his men and before he had time to turn his face toward the enemy— he was struck by the fatal musket ball. He fell from his horse and his sash was stripped from him and used to bear him from the field of battle....The bullet which was said to have been fired by a Tory, entered his back obliquely, just as he turned to wave on his men.... On Friday, May 2nd, he died. On Sunday the funeral was held. It was a quiet affair, although the body was that of a major-general and of a soldier who for courage and patriotism had no superior. [56]

Captain Stephen Rowe Bradley assumed command of Wooster's troops. His company went on to join General Arnold, who was still highly respected; it would be three years until his infamous betrayal. During the battle, a cannonball was fired into the nearby Keeler Tavern.

Not far from the tavern is a memorial to the soldiers from Ridgefield who fought in the battle of 1777. It commemorates "eight Patriots, who were laid in the grounds, companioned by sixteen British soldiers living, their enemies, dying their guests."

Tryon burned several homes in Ridgefield and went on to burn more houses and destroy more supplies in Wilton before making his way to the Saugatuck River and Compo Beach. General Tryon's officers, however, reported fifty to sixty enlisted men and five officers killed or wounded in the two-hour battle at Ridgefield alone.

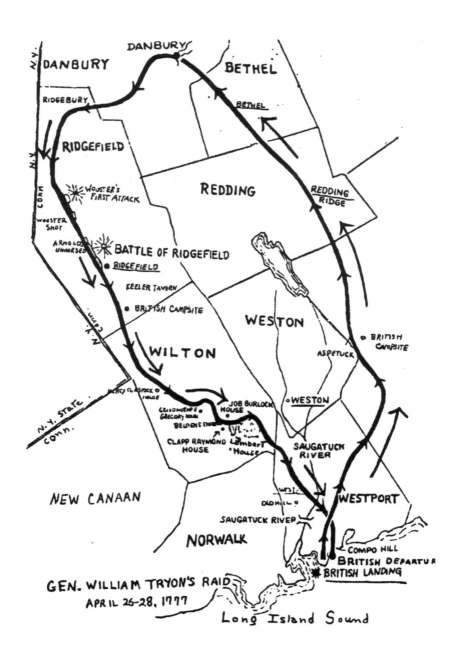

British general William Tryon's raid, April 26–28, 1777.

LOSS OF LIVES AND PATRIOT SUPPLIES

Records obtained from General Howe's official report stated that "in the destruction of the stores at Danbury, the village was unavoidably burnt." He listed the materials lost:

a quantity of ordnance stores, with iron, etc.; 4000 barrels of beef and pork; 100 large tierces of biscuits; 89 barrels of rice; 120 puncheons of rum; several large stores of wheat, oats and Indian corn, in bulk, the quantity hereof could not be ascertained; 30 pipes of wine; 100 hogsheads of sugar; 50 dittos of molasses; 20 casks of coffee; 15 large casks filled with medicines of all kinds; 10 barrels of saltpeter; 1020 tents and marquees; a number of iron boilers; a large quantity of hospital bedding; engineer's, pioneer's and carpenter's tools; a printing press complete; tar, tallow, etc.; 5000 pairs of shoes and stockings.[57]

A committee appointed by the Connecticut General Assembly in May 1777 recorded the losses of nineteen dwelling houses, the meetinghouse of the New Danbury Society and twenty-two stores and barns, with all of their houses consumed. Howe reported British casualties as "one drummer and fife, and 23 rank and file killed; 3 field officers, 6 captains, 3 subalterns, 9 sergeants, 92 rank and file wounded; 1 drummer and fifer and 27 rank and file missing. Royal artillery: 2 additional killed, 3 matrosses and 1 wheeler wounded, and 1 matross missing."

"Return of the rebels killed and wounded" were listed: "Killed: General Wooster; Colonel Gould; Colonel Lamb, of the artillery; Colonel Henman; Dr. Atwater, a man of considerable influence; Captain Cooe; Lieutenant Thompson; 100 privates; Wounded: Colonel Whiting; Captain Benjamin; Lieutenant Cooe; 250 privates. Taken: fifty privates, including several committeemen."

On April 27, 1777, during the Battle of Ridgefield, British troops advanced down Main Street and fired on the tavern because revolutionaries were reported to be making musket balls in the cellar. Today, the tavern is a museum open to the public.

A small cannonball fired on April 27, 1777, is still embedded behind an old shingle on the side of the Keeler Tavern in Ridgefield, Connecticut, as a reminder of the war that was fought there. Viewing the ball is part of a tour. *Courtesy Keeler Tavern.*

A memorial for the Battle of Ridgefield, where eight revolutionaries and sixteen British soldiers were killed.

Chapter 3

Sybil

It was long believed that Sybil's heroic journey remained family legend until 1907, when W.F. Johnson authored a book commissioned and published by two of Henry Ludington's grandchildren, Lavinia Elizabeth and Charles Henry Ludington. The memoirs, originally published for the family, aroused considerable public interest and local pride in Sybil's achievement. In the preface to the memoirs, Johnson states this about the information:

> *The most copious and important data have been secured from the manuscript collections of two of Henry Ludington's descendents, Mr. Lewis S. Patrick [aka Louis], of Marinette, Wisconsin, who has devoted much time and painstaking labor to the work of searching for and securing authentic information of his distinguished ancestor, and Mr. Charles Henry Ludington, of New York, who has received many valuable papers and original documents and records from a descendent of Sibyl Ludington Ogden, Henry Ludington's first born child.*

You can imagine my excitement when I realized that Louis [aka Lewis] S. Patrick wrote an article in the *Connecticut Magazine* revealing the details of the historic ride in 1907 before Johnson, and the article—not the memoirs, as many researchers believed—was the first mention of Sybil's ride. More amazingly, however, was the fact, as I discovered twelve years after the publication of my first book, that Patrick was not actually the first one to go public with Sybil's ride. It was first mentioned in 1880 by a highly respected historian of her time, Martha J. Lamb, as discussed in an earlier chapter, who we now know received her information from Charles Ludington. More on this will be discussed in a later chapter of this book titled "The Fight for Sybil's Rights."

In 1912, Reverend George Noble of Carmel composed a lengthy poem inspired by the information provided by Patrick and Johnson. The poem kept Sybil in the public light but did not gain the fame of Longfellow's poem about Paul Revere.

In 1925, Sybil again reached public attention when a program promoting observances for the sesquicentennial of the American War for Independence began. The goal of the American Scenic and Historic Preservation Society was to mark historical places and objects along or near highways. The society received assistance in Putnam County from the Enoch Crosby Chapter, Daughters of the American Revolution. After hearing Sybil's story from George Turner, a Ludington relative, it was suggested that her ride be marked with New York State Education Department signs. The idea was approved, and dozens of markers were proposed. By 1935, the site of Sybil's home, where she likely began her ride, and her route were clearly marked for public interest.[58]

Berton Braley, a nationally recognized poet, published another poem about Sybil in the *New York Herald Tribune*'s *This Week Magazine* on April 14, 1940. Braley's poem sparked new attention, and Sybil's heroic deed finally caught the public's imagination.

In 1959, internationally renowned sculptor Anna Hyatt Huntington created a bronze equestrian statue of Sybil. It was dedicated on June 3, 1961, in Carmel, New York, Putnam County. A three-foot replica of the statue stands in the plaza of the Danbury Public Library and another at the DAR headquarters in Washington, D.C.

Congressman Robert R. Barry of New York presented an eighteen-inch reproduction of the statue on the grounds of the National Women's Party headquarters on May 18, 1963. Two days later, he addressed the House of Representatives, where he referred to the ceremony: "I place in the Records my remarks made at the unveiling. I would also like to add the text of a ballad entitled, 'The Ride of Sybil Ludington,' written by Mrs. Marjorie Barstowe Greenbie [printed later in this book], and arranged and movingly sung at the ceremony by Mr. and Mrs. Charles Perdue, of Fairfax, Virginia."[59]

Anna Hyatt Huntington (*third from left*) at the statue dedication at Lake Gleneida. *Courtesy Putnam County Historian's Office.*

Barry also shared a resolution made and passed unanimously by the National Women's Party that he then entered in the *Congressional Record* (Vol. 109, No. 75, page A3168):

> *The best tribute we can bring to Sibyl Ludington is to go forward ourselves in the present-day campaign for the complete freedom of American women—with the same courage, the same determination, the same intensity*

ANNA HYATT HUNTINGTON

Anna Hyatt Huntington was a prominent New York City sculptor known for her many sculptures in and around New York City. She was born on March 10, 1876 and died on October 4, 1973. She has the distinction of being a highly successful female artist in a time when women were rarely recognized. Her statue of Joan of Arc, created in 1915, was the first public monument of a woman in New York and the first public New York monument to have been created by a woman. It is not surprising that she is said to have been moved by a poem praising the exploits of a sixteen-year-old female hero of the American Revolution. Huntington was already in her eighties when she created the statue dedicated in 1961 in Carmel, New York, where it was placed on the shore of beautiful Lake Gleneida. Smaller replicas of the statue have been erected at the public library in Danbury, Connecticut; the DAR headquarters in Washington, D.C.; and the Elliot and Rosemary Offner Museum in South Carolina.

of conviction that the heroic young Sibyl Ludington displayed in her famous ride for the freedom of the American colonists from the control of the Government and laws of England.

Be it resolved, therefore, That we send from this gathering a group or spokesman to urge the Senate Committee on Constitutional Amendments, to give its powerful aid, with all possible energy, and all possible speed to bringing final victory, through the passage of the equal rights amendment, the struggle of more than 300 years by American women for complete release from the bondage of the ancient Common Law of England, which largely controls the lives of American women today, even as in still greater degree it controlled the lives of American women in the days of Sibyl Ludington 186 years ago.

Another feather in the young hero's cap came on Tuesday, March 26, 1975, when she rode her way onto a U.S. postage stamp. Ceremonies marking the issuance of the thirty-fifth U.S. stamp to honor a woman drew hundreds of people to Carmel, New York.

With interest in Sybil Ludington aroused, many local newspapers and magazines began writing articles about her historic ride. Two women, Ludmila Ulehla of Long Island and Susan Schefflein of Putnam Valley, created *Sybil of the American Revolution*, an opera performed at the Abigail Adams Smith Museum in New York City on April 1, 1993.

Sibyl's Ride: A Biographical Play about Sibyl Ludington, written by Judy Allen, is performed by children in schools and parks throughout Putnam County. Social studies teachers introduce Sybil to their fourth-grade classes as part of their regular curriculum.

Sybil's rise in popularity created an increasing desire to know more about the teenage hero. However, information about her personal life had been difficult to uncover. To complicate matters, nothing previously published about Sybil was without error, which makes research on Sybil very exciting but sometimes very confusing. Information about her marriage and children, where she lived and how long and even her husband's first name was unclear. A popular biographical piece, "Girl Who Outrode Paul Revere," appeared in *Coronet* in November 1949, but it was woefully incorrect. Its misinformation has been quoted time and again in articles about Sybil:

> *And what became of Sybil Ludington? At 23, she married her childhood sweetheart, Edmond Ogden, and through the years gave him four sons and two daughters. Two of her boys became officers in the Army of the United States. One of them—E.A. Ogden—after serving with distinction through the Blackhawk, Seminole, and Mexican Wars, lived to found Fort Riley, Kansas, where a monument has been erected to him.*

Congressman Barry repeated this paragraph word for word in the *Congressional Record*. Unfortunately, Edmond was not Sybil's childhood sweetheart. She did not have six children, and her son did not "serve with distinction" in any war. In the March–April 1989 issue of *New York Alive*, an article titled "The Midnight Ride of Sibyl Ludington" by Robert W. Pelton quoted the 1949 *Coronet* article verbatim. Historical novels and articles today perpetuate the erroneous information or avoid biographical details altogether.

The source of some misinformation was an error that appeared first in Pelletreau's *History of Putnam County, New York*, published in 1886.[60] It included biographical information about the Ludington children but stated that Sybil married a man named *Henry* Ogden. The list below is as it appeared:

> *Sybil, born April 5, 1761, died 1839, married Henry Ogden;*
> *Rebecca, born January 24, 1763, married Henry Pratt, May 7th, 1794;*
> *Mary, born July 31st, 1765, married David Travis, September 12th, 1785;*

Archibald, born July 5th, 1767;

Henry, 2d, born March 28th, 1769; went to Catskill (his sons, Lewis and Joseph, were the builders of three of the "monitors");

Derick, born February 17th, 1771, died unmarried, December, 1840;

Tertullus, born April 19th, 1773;

Abigail, born February 26th, 1776;

Anna, born March 14th, 1778, married Joseph Colwell;

Frederick, born June 10th, 1782, died July 23d, 1852;

Sophia, born May 16th, 1784, married Mr. Ferris;

Lewis, born June 25th, 1786, died September 3d, 1857;

While this information on the Ludington children was of genealogical interest, it had devastating effects for Sybil researchers. Sybil Ludington never married a Henry Ogden; she married *Edmond* Ogden and had a son named Henry.

Interestingly, Pelletreau added a footnote stating, "A grandson of Sybil, Major Edmund A. Ogden of the United States Army, died at Fort Riley, Kansas Territory, in 1855, where the soldiers under him built a monument to his memory." This information is correct, but many historians and journalists apparently ignored the footnote because they listed Major Edmund A. Ogden as Sybil's *son*. Where did Pelletreau get his information? As is the case with many Sybil "researchers," no sources were given. According to correspondence in Box 1 of MS 2962, he got it from Charles Henry Ludington, which included a handwritten copy of the Colonel's own ledger with the names of his children. Next to Sybil's name was written "Henry Ogden" to indicate her husband's name, an error that haunted Sybil's history for years to come. Her husband was "Edmond" Ogden.

In 1897, J.B. Beers published *A Commemorative Biographical Record of the Counties of Putnam and Dutchess New York* that again listed Sybil's husband as *Henry* Ogden.[61] Beers, however, omitted Pelletreau's footnote about Sybil's grandson, with the result that later researchers, relying on Beers, gave Major E.A. Ogden as Sybil's *son* and not as her grandson—an error that has been repeated in article after article well into the late twentieth century. Neither Beers nor Pelletreau makes mention of Sybil's ride.

In 1907, Willis Fletcher Johnson listed Sybil's husband incorrectly as *Edward* Ogden and didn't include any biographical information on him.[62] There was no mention of Edward's side of the family, but Johnson did mention that there had been an error in the reporting of the name in some previous publications. He notes, "Of these it is further recorded in the same register [he was referring to the register in the ledger kept by Colonel Ludington] that Sybil was married to Edward Ogden (the name is elsewhere given as Edmund or Henry Ogden)."

In a later paragraph about Sybil, Johnson says, "Sybil Ludington, Colonel Ludington's oldest daughter, who married Henry Ogden, a lawyer of Catskill, N.Y. (elsewhere called Edward and Edmund) went to live at Unadilla, N.Y., and bore four sons and two daughters."[63] It is no wonder researchers were confused. Johnson wasn't even consistent with Edmond's name in his own book.

Both Sybil and her father were buried at the Presbyterian cemetery on Maple Avenue in Patterson, New York, beside Abigail Ludington, Sybil's mother. If Johnson had visited the Colonel's grave, he would have noticed Sybil's headstone next to her father's. It reads:

IN
Memory of
SIBBEL
LUDINGTON
Wife of
Edmond Ogden
WHO DIED
Feb. 26, 1839
e. 77 yrs. 10 mo. & 21 ds.

In 1925, Ethel Saltus Ludington in her *Ludington-Saltus Records* confused the issue further by incorrectly identifying Sybil's husband as *Edward* Ogden. *The Yearbook of the Dutchess County Historical Society* in 1940 was partly correct. It correctly listed Major Edmund A. Ogden as her grandson. But it incorrectly stated that she "married October 21, 1784, Edward Ogden, a lawyer of Catskill and left four sons and two daughters."

One of the most surprising pieces of information may be found in *Early Settlers of New York State: Their Ancestors and Descendants* by Janet Wethy Foley, Volume 2, 1934: "Sybil Ludington had but one child, Henry Ogden, and one of her grandsons, Major Edmund Ogden, a distinguished officer of the U.S. Army, died at Fort Riley, Aug. 3, 1855 of cholera. Statements contrary to the above have since been found to be incorrect." Foley was correct, but apparently no one paid attention. Articles continued to claim that she had six children, despite the fact that there are no records to support this.

After researchers in the 1930s realized that Sybil's husband was not named Henry, the confusion it caused was far greater than the simple changing of the name from Henry to Edmond or Edward. Henry was first described as Sybil's husband, and biographical information on him was credited to his father, Edmond. When writers who used Pelletreau and Beers, or even the family memoirs, for information on Sybil's husband reported their findings, it was on Sybil's son Henry and not on her husband Edmond. Henry was the father of six children—four sons and two daughters. Today, researchers may refer to a letter in MS 2962, Box 2, Folder 6 from Sybil's grandson Richard to Lewis Ludington at the New-York Historical Society with a copy of "Family records" from the family Bible. The entry includes birth and death dates for his parents and five siblings and details of his life with his grandmother. He also mentioned letters from George Washington that he had seen in his grandmother's possession that "he fears are now lost." Other letters from each of the other grandchildren are included, with one from E.A. Ogden just months before his death in 1855.

Unfortunately, researchers who believed that Edmond, Sybil's husband, had always been a New Yorker never looked in his Connecticut military records. If they had, they might have uncovered the letters in Sybil's pension file that led to some interesting information about the lives of Sybil and Edmond Ogden, printed in part in a later section of this book.

Sybil Ludington's Ride
by Berton Braley

Listen, my children and you shall hear
Of a lovely feminine Paul Revere
Who rode an equally famous ride
Through a different part of the countryside,
Where Sybil Ludington's name recalls
A ride as daring as that of Paul's

In April, Seventeen Seventy-Seven,
A smoky glow in the eastern heaven
(A fiery herald of war and slaughter)
Came to the eyes of the Colonel's daughter.
"Danbury's burning," she cried aloud.
The Colonel answered, "'Tis but a cloud,
A cloud reflecting the campfires' red,
So hush you, Sybil, and go to bed."

"I hear the sound of the cannon drumming…"
"'Tis only the wind in the treetops humming!
So go to bed, as a young lass ought,
And give the matter no further thought."

Young Sybil sighed as she turned to go,
"Still, Danbury's burning—that I know.
Sound of a horseman riding hard…
Clatter of hoofs in the manoryard…
Feet on the steps and a knock resounding
As a fist struck wood with a mighty pounding.
The door's flung open, a voice is heard,
"Danbury's burning—I rode with word;
Fully half of the town is gone
And the British—the British are coming on.
Send a messenger, get our men!"
His message finished the horseman then
Staggered wearily to a chair
And fell exhausted in slumber there.

The Colonel muttered, "And who, my friend,
Is the messenger I can send?
Your strength is spent and you cannot ride
And, then, you know not the countryside;
I cannot go for my duty's clear;
When my men come in they must find me here;
There's devil a man on the place tonight
To warn my troopers to come—and fight.
Then, who is my messenger to be?"
Said Sybil Ludington, "You have me."

"You!" said the Colonel, and grimly smiled,
"You! My daughter, you're just a child!"
"'Child!'" cried Sybil. "Why I'm sixteen!
My mind's alert and my senses keen,
I know where the trails and the roadways are
And I can gallop as fast and far
As any masculine rider can
You want a messenger? I'm your man!"

The Colonel's heart was aglow with pride.
"Spoke like a soldier. Ride, girl, ride…
Ride like the devil; ride like sin;
Summon my slumbering troopers in.
I know when duty is to be done
That I can depend on a Ludington!"

So over the trails to the towns and farms
Sybil delivered the call to arms
Riding swiftly without a stop
Except to rap with a riding crop
On the soldiers' doors, with a sharp tattoo
And a high-pitched feminine halloo.
"Up! Up there, soldier. You're needed, come!
The British are marching!" and then the drum
Of her horse's feet as she rode apace
To bring more men to the meeting place.

Sybil grew weary and faint and drowsing,
Her limbs were aching, but still she rode
Until she finished her task of rousing
Each sleeping soldier from his abode.
Showing her father, by work well done,
That he could depend on a Ludington.

Dawn in the skies with its tints of pearl
And the lass who rode in a soldier's stead
Turned home, only a tired girl
Thinking of breakfast and then of bed
With never a dream that her ride would be
A glorious legend of history;
Nor that posterity's hand would mark
Each trail she rode through the inky dark,
Each path to figure in song and story
As a splendid, glamorous path of glory—
To prove, as long as the ages run,
That "you can depend on a Ludington."

Such is the legend of Sybil's ride
To summon the men from the countryside,
A true tale, making her title clear
As a lovely feminine Paul Revere!

BERTON BRALEY & WIFE

3694-10

Berton Braley and his wife. *Courtesy of the Library of Congress.*

BERTON BRALEY

Berton Braley (1882–1966) was an American poet with over nine thousand poems to his credit. Most of his poems depict hardworking Americans like Sybil Ludington, who fought for what they believed in. Braley was born in Madison, Wisconsin. Braley was first published at the age of eleven when a small publication printed a fairy tale he wrote. He was a prolific writer, with verses in many magazines. He published twenty books, about half of them poetry collections. For more information, go to www.BertonBraley.com.

The Ride of Sybil Ludington
by Marjorie Barstow Greenbie

Come listen my children and you shall hear,
Of a girl who rode, like Paul Revere,
Long the borders of Connecticut and New York
Where the Yankees stored rations of flour and Pork

We were ready to fight the Redcoats to the ground
If they came from their ships stranded out on the sound,
They, in vain, thought to keep us from being free,
And to keep us in bondage from George 'cross the sea

Colonel Ludington summoned his men and did say,
"Your winter service is over, not to need you I pray,
For we have new recruits who are willing and strong,
to keep the Hudson Highlands you've guarded so long."

"So take up your plough and lay by your guns,
Return to your homes, to your wives and your sons,
Give thanks to the Lord for this moment to seize,
To plant all your crops and to take your ease."

In Danbury now there is food, there is rum,
We've plenty to eat if the Redcoats should come,
There is flour, molasses and bacon in store,
to keep us as we fight them to Hell's own front door.

General Wooster at Ridgefield can stop them cold,
Give them nothing at all to have or to hold,
But at last, long sleep in Connecticut ground
If those Redcoats should land from their ships on the sound.

Sibyl Ludington stood by her father's side,
Sixteen and lovely, the Colonel's own pride,
The eldest of twelve, she had to cook and sew, too
And at home with her family had plenty to do.

But she often found time with the soldiers to spend,
To their joys and sorrows a willing ear she did lend,
As they now were sent back to the homes whence they came,
She spoke to them all and called them by name.

Now Sybil was everywhere cheering the men,
With news of their homes, their family and friends,
She gladdened their hearts with hot coffee and bread,
For the long journey home that she knew lay ahead.

That night in her room o'er a well-filled board,
She and her family gave thanks to the Lord,
For the family was safe, no Redcoats in sight,
And many fathers and sons were home safe that night.

When the rest of her family had gone to bed,
Sibyl at last could rest her tired head,
She lay 'neath the quilt, with her sister, at rest,
And peacefully dozed in the family nest.

She woke with a start at a crashing noise,
At the door below she heard her father's voice,
"The Redcoats in Danbury? Did I hear you right?"
Then she heard a man say, "They surprised us tonight."

"The people are fleeing! The town is aflame!
I spread the alarm along the road as I came."
Then the colonel was saying, "Go muster the men,
We must get them together, our country to defend."

Now Sybil was standing by her father's side,
She saw that the man was too weary to ride,
"Let me go," she said, "to call the men out,
If I get there in time, then the Redcoats we'll rout."

Her father objected to this long hard ride,
Through country where the British deserters might hide.
He knew of the danger and his manner was grave,
When at last his permission to Sybil he gave.

While she dressed and made ready he saddled her steed,
He kissed her goodbye and bade her God-speed,
He gave her a stick to knock at the doors,
She could sound the alarm without leaving the horse.

A murky, spring mist cloaked every star,
and red, to the eastward, dim and far,
The fires of Danbury gloomed on her sight,
As Sybil rode into the soft April night.

But the air was sweet with fresh April smells,
And the voices of peepers like tiny, gold bells,
Made vibrant the night as she skirted the pond,
And searched for the path she knew lay beyond.

She got tangled awhile in briar and brush,
and bogged in a swamp where the grasses grew lush,
But she would save all the people from suffering harm,
so onward she struggled to sound the alarm.

Out of the forest, over hill and through vale,
She raced to Mahopac by way of Carmel,
Then around to Farmer's Mills and back she flew,
Through Stormville to her home—her brave journey was through.

Now Yankees were men not easily ruled,
By hearsay or panic they'd not be fooled,
So some of them acted a little slow,
To pull on their boots and get ready to go.

"I've been roused too often for nothing," one said,
"Why should I leave a good warm bed?"
"Who is it now that's raising a storm?"
"It's the Colonel's daughter Sibyl…she's sounding the alarm."

Forty miles through briars and swamps she has gone,
"So get up and get out…we march at dawn,"
They pulled on their clothes and they got on their gear
Then joining their neighbors, gave Sybil a cheer.

But she was too tired when she got back home,
To realize the worth of the deed she had done,
Four hundred men stood ready to fight,
Where Danbury lay charred in the dawn's early light.

General Tryon awake in the bed of a Tory,
Mission accomplished, but without the glory,
'Midst the chaos and ruin of that fateful night,
His men all lay drunk, not ten fit to fight.

They had found the food for which they had come,
Bacon, molasses, flour and rum,
The molasses ran sticky in every gutter,
They swizzled the rum; burned the bacon and butter.

That's how it was, you all know the rest,
Ludington's men were now at their best,
They fell on the Redcoats, the redcoats retreated,
Their pride in the dust and their plans defeated.

The Yankees harried their rear and then,
Ludington proudly marched forth his men,
To join General Wooster and without pity or plea,
They pushed all the Redcoats back to the sea.

In that year of seventeen seventy-seven,
The people rejoiced and they all thanked heaven,
That the land lay secure in the soft summer light,
And that Sybil Ludington had ridden that night.

Chapter 4

SYBIL AND EDMOND

Sybil Ludington did, in fact, marry Edmond Ogden. He was the sixth child of Humphrey Ogden and Hannah Bennett, who were married in Westport, Connecticut, on November 22, 1743.[64] Hannah was the daughter of Thomas Bennett and Mary Rowland.[65]

Humphrey and Hannah Ogden had eleven children, the first six born in Westport and the last five in Weston, Connecticut. Edmond was born on February 12, 1755 and baptized on July 23, 1755.[66]

At twenty-one years old, he enlisted as a sergeant in a Connecticut regiment and faithfully fulfilled his military duties. His service prompted Sybil, when she was seventy-seven years old, to take advantage of a pension passed as an act of Congress on July 4, 1836. The file may be found in the National Archives in Washington, D.C. (Pension Files, R7777, Ogden, Edmond; Sebal), and is an important primary source of information on the life of Sybil Ludington Ogden.

The file contains, among others, four important letters. In one, signed by Sybil [Sebal] herself, she affirms:

> *The said Cybal* [crossed out and changed to Sybal] *Ogden is the Widow of Edmond Ogden who was a Sergeant in the Army and also in the Navy of the United States in the Revolutionary War and that he the said Edmond Ogden Enlisted at Weston in Fairfield County in the State of Connecticut in the Month of April 1776 as a Sergeant in the Company Commanded by Capt. Albert Chapman in the Regiment Commanded by*

Pension Application File #R7777, Sybil Ogden.

Col. Elmore in the Connecticut Line that he marched with said Company to Albany in the State of New York—thence with said Company and Regiment and under the said Officers he served in the Capacity of a Sergeant at the German Flats at Forts Dayton, Stanwix and other places until the expiration of a term and some days over when he was discharged after, having served over one year as aforesaid in the Northern Campaign he was discharged in the month of April 1777. She the said widow also says that she is under the impression that her said husband served 6 or 8 months in 1778 in the neighborhood of Boston but cannot recollect who the officers were or how long he served in that year—but does further declare and say that she does very well recollect that he her said husband did serve at sea on board several vessels, commissioned by Congress, and particularly under the

Mary Gilbert of the Town of Poughkeepsie in said County, Wife of the Rev Asahel Gilbert, being duly Sworn, deposes & Says, that She is personally acquainted with Sebal Ogden, now a resident of the Town of Unadilla County of Otsego in said Widow, relict of One Edmund Ogden deceased, a revolutionary Officer; who Served in the Naval department of the United States of America Under Commodore John Paul Jones;— that this deponent is a Sister of the Said Sebal Ogden, & the only Sister Surviving;— that this deponent was personally present at the Marriage of the Said Sebal Ogden, her Said Sister, with the Said Edmund Ogden which Marriage was Solemnized before the Expiration of the Revolutionary War, & Several Years previous to the First day of January, in the Year of our Lord One thousand Seven hundred & Ninity Four;— by the Reverend Ebenezer Coles a regularly ordained & esteemed Clergyman of the Baptist Connection—

And this deponent further Says that Said Marriage occurred in the Town of Patterson, in the then County of Dutchess, now Putnam, in the State of New York— And further that the Said Sibal Ogden widow as aforsaid of Said Edmund Ogden is, & has remained a widow ever Since the death of the Said Edmund, who died of the Yellow fever in the City of New York many years ago, since the Year 1800. but in what precise Year this deponent knows not. And further that the Said Sibal is aged, indigent & in very precarious health— Further this deponent Saith not.

Subscribed & Sworn this 21st day August A.D. 1838. Before me Silas C Haight Justice of the Peace in and for Dutchess County—

Mary + Gilbert
her
Mark

State of New York } ss
Dutchess County } This may

Pension Application File #R7777, Mary Gilbert.

command of Paul Jones in the "Bony Richard" [John Paul Jones and the *Bonhomme Richard*] *and other Vessels and Commanders whose names she cannot now recollect but that she does well recollect that her Husband came home from France dressed in French Clothing and that he represented that he had been with Jones on the coast of France, England, and Scotland and that he was with Jones in his hottest battles and that she received letters from him and had one in her possession from him to his father containing a discharge from one of the vessels as Sergeant of Marines which she cannot now find and supposes to be lost.*

It was through this file that some of Sybil's missing life story was finally revealed, and in a sense, this enabled Sybil to tell her own story. Among other things, the file contained a deposition from Sybil's sister Mary Gilbert, wife of Reverend Asahel Gilbert, signed by Bradford Winton, judge of probate for the "District aforesaid," and witnessed by Silas Haight, the justice of the peace of Dutchess County, dated August 21, 1838. In the letter, it was stated that Mrs. Gilbert

is a Sister of the Said Sebal Ogden, and the only Sister Surviving that this deponent [Mrs. Gilbert] *was personally present at the marriage of the Said Sebal Ogden, her Said sister, with the Said Edmond Ogden which marriage was solemnized before the Expiration of the Revolutionary war and several years previous to the first day of January in the Year of Our Lord One Thousand Seven Hundred and Ninety-Four by the Reverend Ebenezer Cole a Regularly ordained and Esteemed Clergyman at the Baptist Connection. And the deponent further Says that Said marriage occurred in the Town of Patterson in the then County of Dutchess, now Putnam in New York.*[67]

Note that Sybil's sister missed their correct wedding date by exactly ten years. When Donald Lines Jacobus quoted Mrs. Gilbert's letter, he omitted the wedding date.

A third letter in the pension files comes from Fanton Burs, then aged "Eighty-two years and over," whose testimony strongly supported Sybil's:

I was a Soldier in the War of the Revolution. That on the fifteenth day of April 1776 I enlisted for twelve months in a Company of I think Connecticut State Troops under the Command of Albert Chapman of Fairfield Town and County and State aforesaid as Capt. in Col. Elmore's

Above: Pension Application File #R7777, Fanton Burs, page 6.

Right: Pension Application File #R7777, Julia (Sybil's sister-in-law), page 4.

Regiment and Marched with said Company to Albany where we joined the Regiment. The Regiment then marched to the German Flatts as called when we built the fort called Fort Dayton. We then marched to Fort Stanwicks where we relieved a Massachusetts Regiment and we continued and finished the fort by them begun and continued at said Fort under the command of said officers untill the 18th day of April 1777 at which time the Regiment was discharged making my time of service one Year and three days—I well remember Edmond Ogden then of Said Town and County of Fairfield and State of aforesaid Enlisting with me into said Company under Said Chapman in Said Col. Elmore's Regiment and went to Albany with me and from there to the German Flatts and from there to Fort Stanwicks and continued there with said Company the full term of one year and three days and was discharged when I was. The said Edmond Ogden enlisted and Served as Sergeant of said Company the whole term aforesaid. He and I were Scholl boys and always very intimate untill he moved into the State of New York. The reason why the company staid over the term of enlistment was in consequence of waiting for the relief guard—
signed
Fanton Burs

The fourth letter, a deposition taken from Sybil's daughter-in-law, Julia Ogden, provides information relating to Sybil and Edmond's later life. Much of the information may also be found abridged in Donald Lines Jacobus's *Families of Old Fairfield*, volumes 1 and 2.

The letters indicate that Edmond and Sybil were not "childhood sweethearts," as many articles suggested. Edmond was born and raised in Connecticut and may not have been anywhere near Sybil while she was growing up. He enlisted in Weston, Fairfield County, Connecticut, in April 1776 and served as a sergeant in Captain Albert Chapman's company and Colonel Elmore's regiment. He served until April 1777—the month of Sybil's ride. When he entered the service, Sybil was fifteen, but Edmond was already twenty-one. After her ride, Sybil remained with her parents until she was twenty-three and helped to raise her brothers and sisters. Edmond was twenty-nine when the Reverend Coles married him and Sybil.

Little is written about Edmond or Sybil in the years before their wedding. However, Johnson, in his memoirs, quotes a passage from an advertisement placed by Colonel Henry Ludington in a local newspaper for land he owned in 1781 in the eastern part of Dutchess County near his home. The passage includes a note about Sybil and her sister. "It was one of the perilous duties of his daughters Sibyl and Rebecca frequently to ride thither on horseback, through the Great Swamp, to see that all was well on the property."[68]

After the war, Colonel Ludington disposed of that land, as the following notice in the *County Journal and Dutchess and Ulster Farmers Register* of March 24, 1789, shows:

> *To Be Sold By The Subscriber:*
> *A Farm of about 104 acres of land in Fredrickstown in the County of Dutchess lying on the east side of the Great Swamp near the place where David Akins formerly lived. There are about thirty tons of the best of English hay cut yearly on such place, and considerable more meadow hay may be made, a sufficient quantity of plow and timber land, a good bearing orchard of the best fruit, a large convenient new dwelling house and a stream of water running by the door. The place is well situated for a merchant or tavern keeper. Whoever should incline to purchase said place may have possession by the first of May next; the payments made as easy as possible and an indisputable title given for the same. For further particulars inquire of the subscriber or Edmond Ogden who keeps a public house on the Premises.*
> *Henry Ludinton*
> *March 9ᵗʰ, 1789*

Although Johnson claims that the land was sold to James Linsley of Connecticut, a deed showing that Sybil and Edmond owned the land is on file at the Dutchess County clerk's office. Johnson's description of the land coincides with the description in the deed:

> *The result of this advertisement was the sale of the farm in question to a man from the former home of the Ludingtons in Connecticut. This appears from a document in the possession of Mr. Patrick, the original of an agreement made on November 5, 1790, between Colonel Ludington and James Linsley, of Branford, Connecticut by which the former covenanted and agreed with the latter to sell a certain farm situate, lying and being in Fredericksburgh butted and bounded as follows adjoining Croton River on the west side and on the south by Abijah Starr and Ebenezer Pabner and on the north by P. Starr & Samuel Huggins. Containing about one hundred and five acres.[69]*

The Ogden family moved to the area in 1783; the Colonel had acquired the land in 1781 and sold it in 1790. On her trips to check out her father's land with Rebecca, Sybil may have encountered Edmond. They were married in 1784.

On October 22, 1779, the state legislature empowered the governor to appoint a commission to take possession of property formerly owned by Royalists. The commissioners handled the liquidation of real estate, and Sybil's father and Benjamin Birdsall acquired 173 acres of land. In 1786, Henry became sole owner of 104 acres of the land. In 1790, he sold the land to James Linsley of Branford, Connecticut. Either Johnson was incorrect about the Linsley sale or Edmond and Sybil purchased the land after 1790 and sold it in 1793.

A deed identifying Edmond Ogden as a farmer and husband of Sybil Ludington and connecting him to Colonel Ludington's 104 acres may be found in the county clerk's office in Dutchess County:

This indenture made the twenty-third day of April one thousand seven hundred and ninety three between EDMOND OGDEN of Frederickstown [Frederickstown was known also as Fredericksburgh] *and County of Dutchess and state of New York farmer and Sybil his wife of the first part and SAMUEL AUGUSTUS BARKER OF Frederickstown aforesaid farmer of the second part witnesseth that the said EDMOND OGDEN and SYBIL his wife for and in consideration of the sum of four hundred and eighty pounds money of the said State to them in hand paid by the said BARKER have and each of them hath granted bargained sold aliened enfeoffed and confirmed and by these do and each of them doth grant bargain sell alien enfeoff and confirm unto the said BARKER and to his heirs and assigns forever ALL that certain tract or parcel of Land scituate lying and being in Frederickstown aforesaid being parcel of a farm of one hundred and seventy three Acres conveyed to BENJAMIN BIRDSALL and Henry LUDINTON* [sic] *by SAMUEL DODGE and JOHN HATHORN Commissioners of forfeiture for the middle district and Lately released to the said HENRY LUDINTON by ABIJAH STAR who purchased of the said BENJAMIN BIRDSALL by certain Deed of partition bearing day the 27th day of May 1786 containing one hundred and four Acres be the same more or less comprehending all the Lands which on the said partition fell to the share of the said HENRY LUDINTON which farm of one hundred and four Acres is intersected nearly in the middle by the road leading from Dover to Danbury and on which said farm is a dwelling house standing on the east side of the said road or highway as the same is divided in a certain deed made between*

THIS INDENTURE made the twenty third day of April one thousand seven hundred and ninety three between EDMOND OGDEN of Fredericks town and County of Dutchess and state of New York farmer and SYBIL his wife of the first part and SAMUEL AUGUSTES BARKER of Fredericks town aforesaid farmer of the second part witnesseth that the said EDMOND OGDEN and SYBIL his wife for and in consideration of the sum of four hundred and eighty pounds money of the said State to them in hand paid by the said BARKER have and each of them hath granted bargained sold alliened enfeoffed and confirmed and by these do and each of them doth grant bargain sell alien enfeoff and confirm unto the said BARKER and to his heirs and assigns forever ALL that certain tract or parcel of Land scituate lying and being in Frederickstown aforesaid being parcell of a farm of one hundred and seventy three Acres conveyed to BENJAMIN BIRDSALL and HENRY LUDENTON by SAMUEL DODGE and JOHN HATHORN Commissioners of forfeitures for the middle district and Lately released

to

Sybil and Edmond
deed.

HERMAN HOFMAN late Sheriff of the County of Dutchess aforesaid and a certain JACOBUS VAN NUYS dated the 8th day of July 1791.[70]

In any case, Sybil and Edmond were married about two years before Henry was born. It would also appear that Edmond was, in addition to being a farmer, an innkeeper in a "public house," an occupation that drew him to the rapidly growing village of Catskill on the Hudson River in Greene County.

The idea of Edmond being an innkeeper is not a new one. In a *Daily Mail* article, dated February 3, 1978, Mabel Parker Smith, the only historian to capture Sybil's days in Catskill, quoted Imer Bellinger, a stepdaughter of a descendant of Colonel Ludington. Bellinger quoted an article by Herb Geller in the *Patent Trader* (Putnam County) on June 9, 1957. In his final paragraph. Geller wrote, "Sybil Ludington never again figured into great events. She married a man by the name of Ogden who kept a tavern near Route 22. She is buried in a churchyard at the Presbyterian Church next to her father who died in 1817 and her mother Abigail who died in 1825."

Geller revealed his source to me as Miss Emma Jane Ludington, one of Sybil's descendants. He warned me that seeing her to verify the story would be impossible since Emma Jane passed on sometime around 1969 or 1970. In any case, Geller and Emma Jane Ludington were right about Edmond's occupation as a tavern keeper.

There is additional evidence that Sybil was still in Dutchess County in the late 1780s. A brief mention of her appears in "A Chronological History of the Presbyterian Church of Patterson-Pawling, New York," compiled by Reverend James B.M. Frost. On page 10, he lists the year 1789 and states:

"Col. Henry Ludington was a trustee of the church. His eldest daughter, Sybil Ludington, and Lt. Col. Ferris were members of the congregation."

The census of 1790 found Sybil and Edmond in Fredericksburgh.[71] They left before the next census was taken. In the Department of Commerce and Labor Bureau of the Census report, "Ogden, Edmund" is listed on page 81 as the head of his household with one other "free white male of 16 years and upward, including heads of family/one free white male under sixteen years/and one free white female including heads of family." While it is not clear who the other "free white male" was living with Sybil and Edmond, it is clear that they only had one male child after seven years of marriage.

The paragraph of the deed below places Sybil and Edmond in Fredericksburgh within three months of a school subscription signed by Edmond in Catskill on August 23, 1793:

> *BE it remembered that on this twenty third day of April in the year one thousand seven hundred and ninety three before me JOHN RAY one of the masters in Chancery for the State of New York personally came EDMOND OGDEN and SYBIL his wife grantors in the within indenture named and the said EDMOND OGDEN acknowledges that he signed sealed and delivered the same as his Voluntary act and deed for the uses therein mentioned and the said Sybil his wife being examined by me privately and apart for her said husband acknowledged, that she signed, sealed and delivered the same as her Voluntary act and deed for the like uses without any fear, threat or compulsion of from or by her said husband and I having perused the same and finding no material erasure or interlinations therein except those noted do allow the same to be recorded—JOHN RAY*
>
> *Recorded this preceading Deed the 13th day of August 1793*
>
> *Beekman Livingston D. Clerk*

Chapter 5

THE CATSKILL YEARS

I n 1792, Sybil and Edmond moved to the village of Catskill on the western shore of the Hudson River, leaving behind the relative peace and quiet of Fredericksburgh. By 1795, Catskill was in a transition period, destined to become a bustling port town: "It had outworn its infant beauty of untouched forest—like a growing child—the white winged sloops that sailed up the Catskill [Creek], the log cabins and log fences, the ox-teams and the wood-roads had something of beauty, but as time passed it grew ungainly, the roads in spring hub-deep with mud, the houses set here and there with little beauty or symmetry."[72] For some there was success, but for others, the dream of a new and easier life never came to fruition. By the late 1790s, Catskill and the Ogdens found themselves facing some difficult years ahead.

The area of most development, The Landing, was situated along Catskill Creek to accommodate commercial traffic drawn to Catskill from western New York. The Landing was located at the foot of Jefferson Hill, below the emerging village where residents of the small community watched processions of farm wagons loaded with produce and livestock making their way to The Landing. Sybil and Edmond and their seven-year-old son, Henry, settled into an environment dominated by the port and its countless activities and diversions. Details of life for the Ogdens in Catskill are sketchy, but county records enable us to follow some of the events of their lives.

A first mention of the Ogdens in Catskill is in James D. Pinckney's *Reminiscences of Catskill*. Edmond was recorded as having subscribed to the academy building fund during the time young Henry was enrolled in a school at The Landing. Such subscriptions were the only means of raising money for a school building. Pinckney discusses the records of subscriptions in papers belonging to Stephen Day dated August 23, 1793: "for the purpose of raising the sum of four hundred pounds, to have an academy erected at The Landing, in said town of Catskill…which sum is to be divided into one hundred shares, computing each share at four pounds." The list of subscribers included "Edmond Ogden." When another subscription was solicited, on May 10, 1795, it was resolved that 120 shares be added. Once again, Edmond bought 2 shares.[73]

There has been some confusion about Edmond's line of work in Catskill. In some sources, he was listed as a lawyer, but there is no evidence to support this. His name was not included in the *History of Greene County* under "Attorneys of the Era." He had been mentioned in 1789 as a keeper of a "public house" in Johnson's memoirs of Colonel Ludington. It is likely that Edmond chose to live in The Landing to make use of his skills. The Ogdens obviously took advantage of this bustling neighborhood to earn their daily bread by catering to the laborers and businessmen who needed food and lodging.

The Ogdens endured as a family until the fall of 1799, when Edmond died, presumably from yellow fever. In her deposition seeking a widow's pension based on Edmond's military service, Sybil stated that "Edmond Ogden died on the 16th day of September 1799." The papers were filed in 1838. At the same time, in another deposition, Mary Gilbert, who was Sybil's only surviving sister, stated that "the Said Sibal Ogden widow; as aforesaid of Said Edmond Ogden, died of the Yellow Fever in the City of New York many years ago circa the year 1800." Julia Ogden, Sybil's daughter-in-law, also deposed that Edmond died in "the month of September 1799." This information establishes the vague outline of where and how Edmond died, but it is most unsatisfying. There is no death certificate, no will and no grave. There was no record of his death in the city's Surrogate Court Office records, and his name is not listed in the New-York Historical Society's archives of people who died of yellow fever at the turn of the nineteenth century. For an unknown reason, Edmond Ogden's death went unnoticed, which is a sad state of affairs for the man who served with John Paul Jones on the *Bonhomme Richard* and eventually wed our hero.

After Edmond's death, Sybil was not alone in The Landing. Her brothers Tertullus and Henry lived nearby. Tertullus was mentioned in an evocative passage revealing a slice of Catskill life from Henry Hill's *Recollections of an Octogenarian*:

> *In the north part of the village were the stores of General Samuel Haight, Andrew Brosnaham, Jacob Klein, Major Hawley, Orrin Day, Benjamin Haxtun and John W. Strong. When Doctor Porter built his house beyond that occupied successively by Jesse Brush, William Brown and Amos Cornwall, it seemed as if he had gone quite out of the village. Looking from his house east to the river, and south to the Point, no building was in sight; and at the top of the hill the old court house and jail, and Olcott's dwelling-house and rope walk stood alone. Across the creek were the houses of Major Cantine, Doctor Benton, and Peter Dubois. South of the shipyard stood that celebrated edifice, the Stone Jug, and large storehouses on the wharves. In or near the lower part of Main Street were Judge Day, Lyman Hall, Joseph Graham and Tertullus Ludington, with their stores, the Widow Ogden and her tavern.* [74]

Not until 1803 does Sybil's name appear again in Catskill records when she applied for an innkeeper's license. That she felt competent to undertake such an occupation strengthens the possibility that she had considerable experience keeping a tavern. What she learned living with Edmond proved to be the mainstay of her economy over the next period of her life. Sybil was listed as an innkeeper in Catskill in 1803—the only female among twenty-three other innkeepers.

By 1804, when Henry was eighteen, Sybil had bought property at the corner of Greene and Main Streets. A deed in the Greene County clerk's office is dated May 4, 1804: "BETWEEN Reuben Webster of the County of Litchfield and State of Connecticut of the one part and Sibel Ogden Widow of the Town of Catskill, County of Greene, State of New York of the other part." The purchase price was "for and in consideration of the sum of Seven hundred & thirty two dollars lawful money of the State of New York to him in hand paid." [75]

Mabel Parker Smith discussed Sybil's purchase in a *Daily Mail* article on January 11, 1978: "By piecing together the evidence of published references such as Beers and Henry Hill with that of property transactions in Greene County land records, it seems safe to assume that the Ogden tavern sign swayed at the southwest corner of Main and Greene Streets for about six years from the purchase of the land." Smith notes further that there was "possibly an erection of a stone structure thereon." But, she continues, "Sybil

Ogden did not serve the public in the present handsome brick residence now occupying the entire Main Street frontage of that corner property running back the length of the Greene block to Hill Street. That she 'improved' the land built on it during her tenure is implicit in the $2275 figure for which she sold this and slight additional land to Lyman Hall in 1810 compared with her own purchase price of $732 in 1804."[76]

Sybil's first year in business was marked by an outbreak of yellow fever. Catskill was hard hit, especially in The Landing, where Sybil's establishment was on Greene and Main. The sickness was all around, and her new venture was certainly hampered by it. Yet she persisted in the face of this adversity. She was a strong woman and held her world together amid chaos. Sybil outlasted the fever and persevered in her chosen profession. J.B. Beers discusses the epidemic in Catskill.

> *Though for general healthfulness the reputation of this locality stands high, the village has on occasions been ravaged by epidemic diseases. The first of these was in 1803, when the yellow fever broke out and for a time raged with much fatality. The epidemic commenced in the month of August. The first two cases occurred on the tenth, the third and the fourth cases on the*

In 1811, Lyman Hall built his home on the property he bought from Sybil Ludington Ogden. It is believed that the foundation was part of Sybil's home and tavern from 1804 to 1810. The house still stands on the corner of Greene and Main Streets in Catskill.

*eleventh, and the fifth and sixth on the nineteenth. The first three cases were
in one family. There were altogether 30 clearly marked cases, and ten or
twelve doubtful ones. One third of them began in August, and the others in
September. Eight persons died, six of whom were males.*[77]

An 1804 medical report written about the epidemic on and around
Greene Street in 1803 is titled "Remarks on the Origin and Progress of
the Malignant Yellow Fever, as It Appeared in the Village of Catskill, State
of New York, during the Summer and Autumn of 1803: In a Letter from
Benjamin W. Dwight to Eneas Monson, M.D. of New Haven, Connecticut."
The letter opens with an important premise: that the commonly held belief
that yellow fever was "never of domestic origin" was wrong. "As Much pains
have been taken, in various newspaper publications, to persuade the people
of this the yellow fever is never of domestic origin, but an imported disease,
I have been induced to state to you some facts which appear to me to support
the contrary."[78]

Some of the doctor's report was repeated and summarized in *The History
of Greene County* by Beers:

*The disease appeared to be confined to that part of the village near the
Hopenose, mainly on Greene Street. On this street there were then several
houses, and on the lower end of it a few stores* [Sybil's brother Tertullus
owned one of these]. *Two or three hundred barrels of herring had been
stored in one of these buildings during the month of the preceding May. A
slaughter yard was then in operation in the village. The effect of it was
so marked that Dr. Croswell claimed that he could tell beforehand, from
its condition and that of the sewer leading from it, in connection with
the weather, whether the families living near it would be visited with the
sickness or not. The water was said to produce diarrhea if freely used. The
people lived very much crowded together, generally two to four families in
each house. These facts indicated bad sanitary conditions, and to them were
attributed the progress of the disease, if not its origin.... Till the present
year, the greatest number of cases has occurred in places considerably remote
from the wharves. The reason is obvious. In addition to the stagnant waters
in the gutters, &c. as above-mentioned, not more than two years ago a
slaughterhouse was opened near the middle of Main Street, a little east from
the road. Here a large number of sheep and meat cattle were slaughtered
during the summer season. All the offals were thrown into the yard, and
lay there from season to season. After every rain, the water which proceeded*

from this yard ran into the street, and there became either partially or wholly stagnant. In the neighborhood of this sink of filth and poison, it has, in several instances, been very sickly. Some cases highly malignant have, at times, occurred. In one small house in particular, so situated as to take more of the stench than any other, Dr. Croswell informs me, that the number of cases of severe sickness, during the existence of this evil, among the several families who have resided in it, have been very remarkable.[79]

In 1805, Sybil was faced with a new dilemma. "Ludington research in Greene County turned up intriguing insights into Sybil's involvement in the business world, as a widow, an independent, emancipated woman neither sheltered nor dominated by a man. A woman alone, suddenly charged with management of her family affairs, she seems to have been caught up in one of the countless speculation and land development schemes which threatened ruin in the young country early in the last century."[80]

Amos Eaton was linked to the "Widow Ogden" in an 1805 land investment scheme involving eighty-four acres in Kiskatom. The land deal eventually resulted in Eaton's conviction for roguery and a sentence to life at hard labor without clemency. Eaton was released, however, after five years and went on to become a pioneer in the teaching and popularization of the natural sciences and the founder of Rensselaer Polytechnic Institute–Troy, under sponsorship of Stephen Rensselaer.

With all she had to do to keep her tavern going, Sybil helped see Henry through his education. He became "Henry Ogden, Att. at law of Unadilla, Otsego County," and married Julia Peck of Catskill. Henry was twenty-four years old when he married. His first son, Edmund Augustus, named for his grandfather, was born on February 20, 1811. After the birth, mother, father, son and grandmother were on their way up the Catskill Turnpike to Unadilla, where Sybil continued to stand by her son for the next twenty-eight years of her life.

Chapter 6

THE UNADILLA YEARS

The Catskill Turnpike, built in the late 1790s, ran from Unadilla to Catskill, and while it first brought business to the Widow Ogden's tavern, in the end it was the path to a new life with Henry and Julia. Unadilla was a place to raise a family in peace and quiet, but it was also a dynamic young community in the rapidly growing area of central New York. In many ways, it was a return to the life Sybil had left behind in Fredericksburgh with her parents.

A description of Unadilla one year before their arrival was included in *The History of Otsego County, New York*:

> *Unadilla rapidly increased in importance…a post-township in the extreme southern angle of Otsego County, thirty-four miles southwest of Cooperstown, and one hundred miles south of west of Albany….The surface is hilly and uneven but along the stream that forms the boundaries, as also some smaller ones, the land is very good and productive….There is a quarry of stones, used for grindstones. There are sixteen saw-mills, that prepare great quantities of lumber for the Baltimore market, descending the Susquehanna in rafts. Five grain-mills, an oil-mill, and some waterworks, besides five distilleries of whiskey. There is one Episcopal church and fourteen schoolhouses, in which school is kept part of the year….The whole population is 1,426, with 116 senatorial electors, 344 taxable inhabitants, and $141,896 of taxable property.* [81]

Ironically, Otsego County was once part of Tryon County, named for colonial governor William Tryon, the same man who burned Danbury in 1777, forcing Sybil to muster her father's troops against him. Sybil Ludington was not recognized as a hero in Otsego County. Her years there were spent in almost complete obscurity as "the Widow Sybil Ogden" and as "the mother of Henry Ogden, Att. at Law." There are no headlines for her achievements, no plaques and no roadside markers. She is not even buried there; her body was returned to Dutchess (now Putnam) County and buried beside her parents behind the church built by the congregation she was a member of as a child. Today, the letters from her grandchildren shed a new light on Sybil's life in Unadilla.

The Catskill Turnpike was a well-traveled thoroughfare to central New York, according to the *Unadilla Times*, and it remained so for a quarter of a century.[82] Two stages were kept regularly on the road, charging a fare of five cents per mile. A stage left Catskill on Wednesday morning and reached Unadilla Friday night. It is likely that one Wednesday morning in 1811, Sybil Ludington Ogden, with her son, Henry; his wife, Julia; and their child, Edmund Augustus, boarded one of those coaches and headed for Unadilla, an important market town and a thriving inland port where a young attorney could make a name for himself and rise to prominence.

Henry was quite the country gentleman in the little town at the end of the turnpike. In style, respect and dignity, life for the Ogdens bore many similarities to the life of the Fredericksburgh Ludingtons. Sybil helped to raise her siblings in Fredericksburgh much the way she helped to raise six grandchildren in Unadilla and suffered with them the heartaches that mothers and grandmothers know only too well. One of the children, her granddaughter Mary, died at fifteen years old.[83] In her deposition to the military pension review board dated August 8, 1838, Julia Ogden deposed that she was "personally well acquainted with the Widow Sibal Ogden of Unadilla—that she, the said Julia is Daughter-in Law to the said Sibal Ogden that they have lived in the same house together about thirty years past."[84]

A further documentation of Sybil's presence in Unadilla comes from Frances Whiting Halsey's *The Pioneers of Unadilla Village 1784–1840*. The Ogdens are mentioned throughout the book, but in particular as part of a description of the village as quoted from an article in the *Times*:

> *Next was the law office of Henry Ogden, Esq., occupying the site on which afterward was built by Rufus Mead the store now standing vacant. The office was moved down near the mills and altered into a dwelling. Next was the residence of Henry Ogden and Family, consisting of himself, his*

mother, his wife, four sons and two daughters, occupying the site of the present Episcopal rectory.[85]

The most interesting evidence of Sybil's residency in Unadilla, however, came for me when I was searching Revolutionary War pension records for proof of Colonel Ludington's participation in the Danbury affair. In application #S 23152 for Jonathan Carley, I found confirmation of Sybil's residency in Unadilla (quoted earlier in this book).[86] Carley was "formerly of South East town, Dutchess County, New York, until about twenty years after the war when he moved to Sidney, Delaware County, New York." The application contains a letter signed by Sybil confirming her residence in Unadilla just six years before her death on February 26, 1839. Sidney is several miles from Unadilla. (The Carley deposition is also discussed further in a later section of this book.) "Sybil Ogden of the town of Unadilla in the County of Otsego—aged seventy-three years—being duly sworn, says…"

A final confirmation of Sybil's residence in Unadilla appears at the top of her own application for a widow's pension in file #R7777 signed on September 8, 1838:

> *Be it known that on the eighth day of September in the year Eighteen hundred and thirty eight personally appeared before me, Hiram Kinne, one of the judges of the County Court in and for the County of Otsego being Courts of second—the widow Cybal (changed to Sebil) Ogdin a resident of the Town of Unadilla in Otsego county in the state of New York—aged seventy-seven years last April who being first duly sworn according to Law doth on her Oath make the following declaration.*

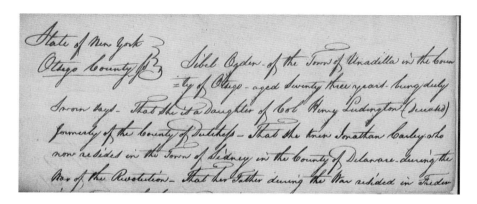

Top of Jonathan Carley deposition S23152.

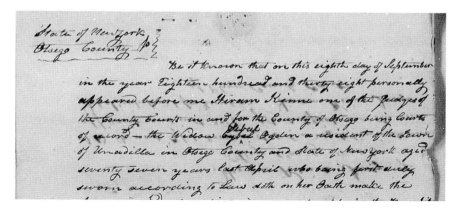

Top of page 2 of application from Sybil's file #R7777.

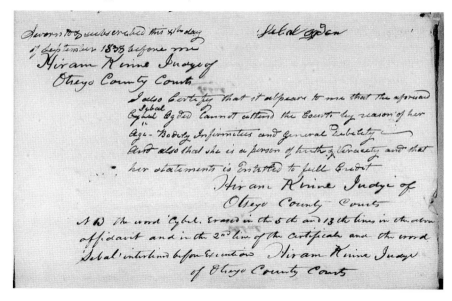

Bottom of page 3 of application from Sybil's file #R7777.

It is also important to note that Sybil's health deteriorated considerably after her presence in court for the signing of the Jonathan Carley pension application on February 1, 1834. At the bottom of his letter in September 1838, Judge Kinne stated: "I also certify that it appears to me Cybal (changed to Sebal) Ogdin cannot attend the courts by reason of her age—bodily infirmities and General Disability—and also that she is a person of truth and Veracity and that her statement is Entitled to full Credit."

Kinne also noted as a footnote: "The word Cybil erased in the 5th and 13th lines in the above affidavit and in the 2nd line of the certificate and the word Sebal interlined before Execution."

It should also be noted that Sybil passed away on February 26, 1839, five months after signing this letter.

For many years, it was believed that the office building and the house the Ogden family had occupied had long been torn down, but both Henry Ogden's office building and his house were kept intact well into the late 1900s. Each was moved on logs to a new location. The office building became part of the William Sewell home. A feature of the rear of the house was a small Masonic symbol, evidently put there by Henry Ogden himself, an active Mason. The LeFever family, who owned the building, donated the wooden symbol to the Unadilla Masons.

Sybil's son and daughter-in-law had four sons and two daughters:

- Edmund Augustus was born in 1811 and died in 1855 at Fort Riley, Kansas.
- Henry A. was born in 1813; died on August 30, 1853; and was buried on December 11, 1854.[87]
- Mary was born in 1818 and died on August 19, 1833, at fifteen.
- Emily was born in 1820; died on October 9, 1841, at twenty-one; and was buried on July 26, 1849 (brought from Maryland).[88]
- Richard (1822–1900) lived in California after serving in the army.
- Frederick (1826–1880) also later resided in California.

In recent research, I have been able to track down each of Sybil's grandchildren (see Sybil's family tree). Letters from several of the grandchildren mentioned below can be found in file MS 2962 in the New-York Historical Society Library Research Center.

Colonel H. Ludington 1739–1817	m 1760	Abigail Ludington 1745–1825
Sybil Ludington 1761–1839	m 1784	Edmond Ogden 1755–1799
Henry Ogden 1786–1837	m 1810	Julia Peck (6 children) 1790–1849

1. Edmund A. Ogden (1811–1855) <u>m</u> 1835 Eliza Loomis (1818–1899)*
(8 children)
 1. Julia Ogden (1839–1840)
 2. Henry L. Ogden (1843–1860)
 3. Edmund Augustus Ogden Jr. (1845–1865)
 4. Gustavas Ogden (1846–1846)
 5. Eliza Emily Ogden (1848–1876)
 6. Isabella Ogden (b. 1850)
 7. Kate Fauntelroy Ogden (1852–1908) <u>m</u> Edwin Booth 1879
 8. Edith Panton Ogden (1854–1890)

*Eliza Loomis Ogden remarried 1862 John M. Ganesvoort after Edmund's death in 1855.

2. Henry A. Ogden (1813–1853) <u>m</u> Elizabeth Ganesvoort
(1 child)
 Henry Ganesvoort (1852–1930)

3. Mary Ogden (1818–1833)
(none)

4. Emily Ogden (1820–1841)
(none)

5. Richard Ogden (1822–1900) <u>m</u> 1854 Isabel Pratt (1835–1911)
(2 children)
 1. Isabelita Ogden (1855–1924) <u>m</u> 1883 Richard Henry Pease (1848–1919)
  Richard Henry Pease Jr. (1886–1929)
  Mary Lita Ogden Pease (1884–1934) <u>m</u> Arthur Barry Watson (1880–1927)
   John B. Watson (1906–1988) <u>m</u> Katrine Breuner (1909–1990)
    Sallie Cluff Watson (1936–2001) <u>m</u> John W. Stark (1934–2005)
 2. Jeanie Antoinette Ogden (1859–1941) <u>m</u> 1884 Samuel Abbot IV (1855–1936)
  Samuel Abbot V (1890–1963) <u>m</u> 1914 Martha Kittle Foster (1891–1987)
   Samuel Abbot VI (1917–1962) <u>m</u> 1940 Myra May Hall (1918–2003)
    They had 2 sons and 3 daughters, including Samuel Abbot VII

6. Frederick Ogden (1826–1880)
(none)

Edmund Augustus graduated from West Point and served the army in the Black Hawk (Florida) and Mexican Wars. He died a respected brevet major at Fort Riley, Kansas, in 1855 and is buried in Unadilla (see sidebar). New information about each of Sybil's grandchildren has been revealed in the letters in Box 1 of the Ludington Family Papers, MS 2962. Richard, who later resided in California and became a commodore, served in the army as a captain and assistant quartermaster.[89] His brother Frederick also made his home in California and died there. Mary was born in 1818 and died in Unadilla in 1833. Emily was the family's second loss; she died in Maryland in 1841.

Life for Henry was very active in Unadilla and, as stated earlier, bore a remarkable resemblance to the life of Henry Ludington. Henry was named for his grandfather much the way his son was named for his grandfather. Both Henrys were active in their respective churches: Henry Ogden was a member of St. Matthew's vestry for many years, and Henry Ludington served on the board of trustees for the Presbyterian Church of Patterson.[90] They both held public office, and both men served in the New York State Assembly.[91] Henry Ogden was also an active member of the Masons and a member of the Susquehanna Bridge Company, created to serve Unadilla. He was one of his village's first trustees and became commissioner of schools in 1826 and again in 1830.[92] While Henry Ludington was associated with names like George Washington and Rochambeau, Henry Ogden was associated with names like Gouverneur Kemble, Washington Irving and James R. Paulding.[93]

EDMUND AUGUSTUS OGDEN

A study of Sybil Ludington's life would not be complete without mention of Edmund Augustus Ogden, himself a hero who was also cheated by history. While his grandmother was forgotten for more than 120 years, Edmund was honored at the time of his death and then forgotten.

Sybil was with her grandson from birth until the time he left to become a West Point cadet, and she had reason to be proud of his distinguished career in the army. In his memoir, Johnson reprints Edmund's obituary from the *New York Observer*, October 18, 1855:

Major Edmund A. Ogden, of the United States Army…died of cholera at Fort Riley, Kansas Territory….On graduating [from West Point], Edmund A. was attached as Brevet Second Lieutenant to the First Regiment of Infantry, then stationed at Prairie Du Chien. He was subsequently appointed a First Lieutenant in the Eighth

Edmund Ogden.

Infantry, where he served until appointed a Captain in the Quartermaster's department, in which corps he remained until his death. He served with credit and distinction through the Black Hawk, Florida, and Mexican Wars, and was created a Major by brevet, for meritorious conduct in the last named of these wars....For the last six years previous to last spring [1849–55], Major Ogden was stationed at Fort Leavenworth, where he has rendered important service to the army in his capacity of Quartermaster. From this post he was ordered to California, and he removed with his family to New York with the expectation of embarking on the 20ᵗʰ of April last, when his orders were suddenly suspended, and he was sent back to assist in outfitting the expedition against the Sioux Indians. He was afterward charged with the arduous duty of erecting, within three months, barracks, quarters, and stables for a regiment of troops at Fort Riley—a point about 150 miles west of Leavenworth, and which he had himself selected as a suitable place for a government post, when stationed at Fort Leavenworth. This place was not settled and was an almost perfect wilderness. He took with him about five hundred mechanics and laborers, with tools [and] provisions, and commenced his labors. In a new and unsettled country, so destitute of resources, many obstacles were encountered, but just as they were being overcome, and the buildings were progressing, cholera in its most fatal and frightful form, made its appearance among the men, from two to four of them dying every day. Far removed from home and kindred, and accustomed to depend on Major Ogden for the supply of their daily wants, they turned to him in despair for relief from the pestilence. He labored among them night and day, nursing the sick and offering consolation to the dying. At last the heavy hand of death was laid upon him, and worn out with care, watching, and untiring labors, he fell victim to the disease whose ravages he had in vain attempted to stay.[94]

It is interesting to note the estimation in which Major Ogden was held at Fort Riley. Johnson quotes from an article in the *Kansas Herald*:

The death of Major Ogden left a deep gloom upon the spirits of all the men, which time does not obliterate. His tender solicitude for the spiritual and bodily welfare of those under him, his unceasing labors with the sick, and his forgetfulness of self in attendance upon others, until he was laid low, have endeared his memory to everyone there. And, as a affection, they are now engaged in erecting a fine monument which shall mark their appreciation of the departed. The monument, which will be of the native stone of the locality, is to be placed on one of the high promontories at Fort Riley and can be seen from many a distant point by those approaching the place. [The plaque will say] *Erected to the memory of BREVET MAJOR E.A. OGDEN, The founder of Fort Riley; a disinterested patriot and a generous friend; a refined gentleman; a devoted husband and father and an exemplary Christian. Few men were more respected in their lives, or more lamented in their deaths. As much the victim of duty as of disease, he calmly closed a life, in the public, distinguished for integrity and faithfulness.*

The revered soldier was quickly forgotten, however. W.F. Pride tells of the fate of Edmund Ogden's monument in *The History of Fort Riley* (1926):

The stone was of the kind used in the building of Fort Riley. In time, neither the government nor anyone else heeding it, cattle made it a rubbing post, vandals chipped pieces from it and scratched their names on it and it became a wreck....Another shaft was afterward erected, much better than the original....This, too, was neglected—left a rubbing post for cattle after the wooden fence around it rotted down....In 1887, General James Forsyth, then Colonel of the 7th Cavalry, took command of Fort Riley....He secured a small allowance from the quartermaster's department, with which, and some labor within his control, he had it repaired—scratches worked out and a permanent iron fence put around it.[95]

And so it seems that Sybil's grandson was remembered in Kansas. He was buried in the Episcopalian churchyard in Unadilla only feet away from where he undoubtedly played as a child, beneath a headstone now weathered and difficult to read. The gravestone is the only memorial to him in Unadilla. Dedicated by his friends in Kansas, it reads:

To the Memory of
Major Edmund Augustus Ogden
of the U.S. Army
Born at Catskill. N.Y. 1811.
Died at Fort Riley Kansas Territory, August 3, 1855

The friends who were with him during the last years of his professional life and near him at his death have asked the privilege of raising this monument wherein to record their honor for him as a citizen and soldier, their love for him as a Christian and a man and to tell how faithful to the last he was to humanity, how true to all his obligations.

In all, Sybil Ogden and her son, Henry, came a long way together from their days in Catskill. From the death of her husband, Edmond, through unquestionably tough business years and until the day her son died a husband and father of six children, Sybil Ludington never left his side. Details of Sybil's last years in Unadilla are recounted in letters to her brother Lewis and her grandchildren in the MS 2962 collection at the New-York Historical Society.

In a letter from Sybil to her brother on January 23, 1838, a year before her death on February 26, 1839, she wrote:

> *I assume you have not heard of the melancholy intelligence of my son Henry's death, he died on the 27th day of November last—He suffered a great deal of pain through his last sickness but was very patient through it all, had his senses perfectly and closed his own eyes—this bereavement my Dear Brother has been a sad and sorrowing affliction to me. It has taken away my last stay and comfort in this world and left me in [illegible]. A lone widow without a child to smooth and comfort my few remaining days to the grave. I thought I should have gone before him but Providence has ordered otherwise and now I must bow in submission to the final stroke and wait with patience the time when God shall also call me to my account— My son has left his business in a very unsettled state and what will be the closing of his concerns I am not able to tell. The family will probably be left in straitened circumstances and as for myself I shall be destitute of a home in the Spring and what is to be my end, divine Providence only knows. If I can be placed in a situation to be made comfortable the little time I have to live I hope I shall be thankful and pray I have strength to sustain me in whatever trials may await me—*
>
> *My Kindest regards to all of your family and believe me Dear brother*
> *Your very affectionate*
> *Sister Sebel Ogden*

Perhaps the greatest irony in Sybil's life story involves the pension application papers she submitted to the War Department in 1837 in an attempt to aid her family. Today, these papers are essential documents, enabling us to know more about her, but Sybil's request was rejected. She couldn't produce her marriage certificate and was therefore denied compensation for her husband's service to his country.

Sybil's rejection letter from the War Department.

Sybil Ludington was a Revolutionary War hero who was little known for a deed that contributed to her country's history. But she was more. Sybil was a lady in a war and time when women were not remembered well, and she lived a life that should not be forgotten. She fended for herself when her husband died, raised a son against all odds and stood by him as he became a man of prestige and honor—a lawyer, an assemblyman and a father of six children, one a West Point graduate who later became a hero. The Ludingtons and Ogdens of the eighteenth and nineteenth centuries are gone—but we can keep them from being forgotten. With new information on Sybil, we can give this extraordinary woman the place in history she rightly deserves. It is my hope this extended biography will contribute to the fight for Sybil Ludington's right to be remembered for who she was in the time and place she lived and died.

Chapter 7

THE FIGHT FOR SYBIL'S RIGHTS

The most difficult part of my recent research on Sybil Ludington has been debunking the debunkers. There are those who believe that Sybil's ride simply did not take place; they debunk her story as mere legend. One of her skeptics took me by surprise with a blog written in June 2006.[96] After a review of research on Sybil, the blogger states, "In short, I have to classify the story of Sybil Ludington as legend, not a documented Revolutionary event."

He continues in a later blog with: "The thin evidence in Johnson's book [Willis Fletcher Johnson's *Colonel Henry Ludington: A Memoir*] and elsewhere hasn't stopped twentieth-century Sybil Ludington fans from spinning off new statements about her....But does any version cite sources for that information that go back more than one century?"[97]

In a mission to set the record straight, I began digging through my research to find ways to address the blogs and defend my teenage heroine. I knew I needed to find more documentation. On November 3, 2006, the blogger was back online with more on Sybil. This time he quoted from Willis Fletcher's memoirs as I quoted them earlier in this book. After quoting Johnson's passage on Sybil's ride, the new blog stated:

> *Already we see the poetic language, the dire details, the emphasis on a lone young female, and the comparison to Paul Revere—all hallmarks of the Sybil Ludington legend in the decades to come. But we don't see any sources specified for this episode, anywhere in the book. Furthermore, as I discussed before, Johnson was a journalist for hire, his book was published by the*

Ludington family itself, and this first version of Sybil's story dates from 125 years [actually 130] after the event it describes. So as a historical authority, this passage is the equivalent of me telling you about something very heroic one of my relatives did in 1881 with no documentation.[98]

Fortunately for Sybil fans, new information brought to the surface a third mention of Sybil's ride. On January 14, 2012, Kevin Gilbert, who blogs under the name "Samuel Wilson," revealed information reported by Martha J. Lamb, former editor of the *Magazine of American History*, who wrote about Sybil Ludington in the 1880s on page 158 and 159 of her *History of the City of New York: Its Origin, Rise, and Progress*. The book had apparently been digitized by Google Books in 2010, and Sybil's ride is mentioned here without some of the additional information offered by Willis Fletcher Johnson and Lewis S. Patrick in 1907. Lamb wrote:

Late in the evening a flying messenger for aid reached Colonel Ludington in Carmel, New York, whose men were at their homes scattered over the distance of many miles; no one being at hand to call them, his daughter Sibyl Ludington, a spirited young girl of sixteen, mounted her horse in the dead of night and performed this service, and by breakfast-time the next morning the whole regiment was on its rapid march to Danbury. But the mischief had been accomplished. The British apprised of the approach of the Americans in the early morning of the 27th, burned all the dwelling houses in the town and retreated upon the Fairfield road towards the sound.[99]

Lamb's quote then continues to discuss the battle that ensued, and the blogger was back with the conclusion that "this makes the Sybil Ludington legend a *little* more credible" and bulleted the following:

There's only a 103-year lag between the ride and the earliest known written description of it, instead of 125 years. Lamb published for a national readership while Johnson published for the Ludington family, an uncritical audience. Lamb didn't claim that Sybil's ride turned out to be important, which fits the contemporaneous record. The Danbury raid was a success for the British army and there still doesn't seem to be any record of Col. Ludington's militia unit getting into the fight.

The blogger ends by saying he is "still skeptical until more solid evidence turns up."[100]

I must say that the third blog made me feel somewhat more secure in my defense of Sybil's case. If the notation from Lamb was 103 years after the ride, it made it only 41 years after her death, and perhaps earlier, since Lamb needed time to do the research. Lamb's report was almost in Sybil's lifetime. It is also important to note that Lamb did not use any "poetic language, the dire details, the emphasis on a lone young female, and the comparison to Paul Revere" that the blogger seemed to object to in Johnson's description of the ride. Lamb simply reported that Sybil sounded the alert because no one else was available to do it.

It is unlikely that Martha Lamb spoke with Sybil herself. Lamb was born on August 13, 1829; she was only nine years old when Sybil died on February 26, 1839. It is, however, possible that her *source* was very much alive in Sybil's life span. Could it have been Lewis S. Patrick as stated earlier in this book? Lamb did not credit a source for her information, and a trip to the New-York Historical Society to go through her notes offered me no clues at the time of my visit on August 22, 2012. However, a second visit on November 21, 2017, did reveal a mention of a "Mrs. Ludington" in a letter to Lamb from an "E.A. Smith." At the time, I had no idea that this very library had the information I had been searching for; it just was not in the Lamb files. While the letter did not offer information about Sybil's ride, it did acknowledge the fact that Martha Lamb knew of a "Mrs. Ludington" in the 1870s. We then assume that her information about the ride came from this family member and not a reliable primary source. Or that the source was not quoting from a primary source. Or we revert to the memoirs that recount a story told and discussed at family reunions while the Colonel and Abigail were still alive to tell them, stories collected by their historian descendants, Lewis S. Patrick and Charles H. Ludington.

Willis Fletcher Johnson spoke of his information for his memoir on Colonel Ludington as being

> *gleaned from many sources, including Colonial, Revolutionary and State records, newspaper files, histories and diaries, correspondence, various miscellaneous manuscript collections,* and some oral traditions of whose authenticity there is substantial evidence. *The most copious and important data have been secured from the manuscript collections of two of Henry Ludington's descendants, Mr. Lewis Patrick of Marinette Wisconsin, who has devoted much time and painstaking labor to the work of searching for and securing authentic information of his distinguished ancestor, and Mr. Charles Henry Ludington of New York, who has received*

many valuable papers and original documents and records from a descendant of Sybil Ludington Ogden, Henry Ludington's first-born child.[101]

I can now tell you that those "original documents and records from Mr. Charles Henry Ludington of New York" *do* exist at the New-York Historical Society Research Center, and the source of Martha Lamb's information is now known. Much easier to pursue, however, was the blogger's comment about there not being any record of Colonel Ludington's militia unit getting into the fight. After a tedious search of dozens of pension records from members of Colonel Ludington's troops who took part in the Danbury affair, I was able to pinpoint eyewitness accounts and depositions mentioning Colonel Ludington's troop involvement in defending Connecticut during General Tryon's raid. A great find was the pension application for James Mead, NY application W.1911, page 6:

> *On the 25th day of October in the year 1832 personally appeared before Henry Wynkoop one of the judges of the County court in and for said county of Ulster, James Mead, a resident of the Town of Shandaken, County of Ulster and State of New York aged 77 who first duly swore doth on his oath made the following declaration in order to obtain the benefit of the Act of Congress proposed the 7th of June 1832.*[102]

Among other things, Mead deposed that "he was frequently called out on alarm the first for the term of two weeks at the time Danbury was burnt by the British army in Captain Joel Mead's company, Col. Luddington's [*sic*] regiment."

Another such find was in the application papers of David Mead.[103] According to page 6 of New York Pension Application Record S.9975, David Mead, of Genesee County, on October 16, 1832, appeared before an Open Court of Common Pleas at the age of seventy-five and was duly sworn under the scrutiny of law, on his oath, to make a declaration in order to obtain the benefit of the act of Congress as proposed on June 7, 1832.

Among other things, page 6 of the deposition states:

> *Early the next spring this declarant removed from North Castle to Fredericks Town a distance of 15 or 30 miles easterly of Fishkill where he resided a little more than two years—In the spring following he marched with a company of Militia from Fredericks Town under command of Captain Joel Mead of Litchfield in Connecticut to intercept the British on their*

Pension Application File #S9975, David Mead.

*retreat from Danbury—they united with other companies near Compo
Point in a regiment commanded by Colonel Henry Luttenton* [corrected
to read Ludington] *where they had a pretty smart skirmish with British
soon after which he saw troops return home to Frederickstown taking no
discharge but a hard one—having been absent only 3 or 4 days.*

Another deposition comes from Ezra Ferris, application W.16987, who,
on October 16, 1832, at seventy-two years old in Genesee County, State of
New York, deposed:

*That in the month of December, 1776, this despondent resided in a place
called Fredricksburgh precinct in the county of Dutchess, State of New
York and volunteered as one of the militia of said State in the Company
of Capt. Henry Joel Mead in the regiment of Col. Henry Luddington—
That in the Spring of Seventeen Seventy Seven he was a volunteer in
the military from the same company under Capt. Mead and in Col.
Luddington's regiment marched to Ridgefield and arrived there at the time
Gen. Wooster was killed in the skirmish at that place after Danbury was
burned that he marched from there to Kompo [Compo] when the British
reembarked.*[104]

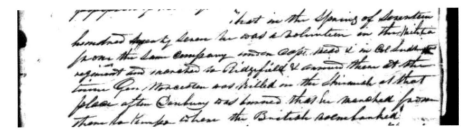

Pension Application File #W16987, Ezra Ferris.

And yet a fourth account came from Alexander McLeod, Application S11052, one of Colonel Ludington's troops who was involved in the Danbury affair, who on August 25, 1832, personally appeared before John Willard, first judge of the Court of Common Pleas of the County of Washington of the Town of Argyle, at the age of seventy-seven. McLeod declared that

> *he enlisted for 6 months on or about the first of May in the year 1777 at Fredericksburgh in Dutchess County, in the company commanded by Captain Calkins in the regiment commanded by Colonel Henry Ludington in the line of the State of New York, in the State service—was in the engagement at Ridgefield in the State of Connecticut when the enemy came to burn Danbury, sometime in the month of May 1777* [it was actually the end of April] *when General Wooster was killed.*[105]

Another discovery in my research was found in a book written by Stephen Darley, *Call to Arms: The Patriot Militia in the 1777 British Raid on Danbury*[106] (not to be confused with my own book, *Sybil Ludington: The Call to Arms*). Darley obviously spent a good deal of time reading through the pension applications. His book was a treasure-trove of information about Sybil. Among his other great finds, he discovered a mention of Sybil's ride prior to 1907. On page 480 of the *National Magazine* for April 1893 was an article written by Howard Louis Conard on Nelson Ludington, a nephew of Colonel Ludington, who stated the following:

> *In Lamb's* History of New York *it is stated that he* [Colonel Ludington] *frequently thwarted the designs of the British General Howe in consequence of which a price was set on his head, and on one occasion, when the Tories had surrounded his home, his capture was only prevented by the bravery and presence of mind of his daughters Sibyl and Rebecca*

Pension Application File #S11052, Alexander McLeod.

Ludington who "were standing guard with guns in their hands" and discovered the enemy in time to ward off danger by a clever ruse. It was the first named of these daughters whose all-night ride on horseback to arouse Col. Ludington's regiment of "minute men" just after the British forces had raided Danbury, Connecticut is hardly less famous than the midnight ride of Paul Revere. [107]

What Darley did not specify in his book was that Conard's quote actually came from Martha Lamb's *History of the City of New York* in 1880, which we now know came from the Colonel's grandson Charles H. Ludington in 1854, 1878 and 1879 and did not include information from his letter about Sybil's ride to alert General Putnam of the raid on Danbury. Conard—an Ohio State librarian (1883–85) credited with editing the *Encyclopedia of the History of Missouri, a Compendium of History and Biography for Ready Reference* in 1901— unfortunately did not offer references for information on Sybil because Lamb did not offer any, but we must note that Conard trusted Lamb's information enough to include it in his article. We must also note that Conard was the first to compare Sybil's ride with that of Paul Revere, a correlation later repeated by Lewis S. Patrick in his article in *Connecticut Magazine*.

In chapter 3 of his book, Darley refers to many of the pension records documenting the involvement of Colonel Ludington's troops in the Danbury raid. Although he does not mention Alexander McLeod, he does mention James and David Mead; Ezra Ferris; Captain Nathaniel Scribner; and Privates Noah Robertson, John Porter, Joshua Gregory, Elisha Dakin, Elisha Gifford, Charles Townsend, Reuben Ganong, Amos Kniffen and William Drew.

I should tell you here that I do not know why Charles Henry Ludington altered his story from its original version. Perhaps the answer is in the missing files of Lewis S. Patrick. In any case, we now have a letter written from 1854 from a grandson of Colonel Ludington, son of Lewis Ludington, a member of Sybil's immediate family. Whether the mention of Sybil's ride was fifty miles round trip to General Putnam or forty miles to muster her father's troops closer to her home, she apparently made a dangerous ride through parts of the Hudson River Valley at the risk of her life. And whether she saved her father with her sister or her mother, or both, she saved the life of an important American officer. My question to naysayers is whether saving the life of a Patriot as important as Colonel Ludington and acting as his sentinel, ride aside, would be considered heroic enough to warrant Sybil the designation of National Patriot. As for *only* family hearsay, the family members were the primary witnesses to the event and shared their stories with their own immediate families. Until they were questioned by Charles H. Ludington and Lewis S. Patrick, they simply were not asked to share their family knowledge of the ride or Sybil.

Chapter 8

THE HUNT FOR ANSWERS

As moving and thought-provoking as I found the blogs and Darley's book to be, I was also pleased by a well-researched article published in the *New England Quarterly* on May 7, 2015 (vol. 88, no. 2, pages 187–222). The article, titled "Sybil Ludington, the Female Paul Revere: The Making of a Revolutionary War Heroine," by Paula D. Hunt, is an amazing comprehensive look at Sybil and her ride.[108] Although not a debunker herself, Hunt does address skepticism of Sybil and offers some sound arguments as to why Sybil is still a hero for many and yet dismissed by others.[109] The article prompted me to locate Paula D. Hunt by telephone on July 10, 2018, to verify some of her information and discuss her position on Sybil Ludington.

Her article began with a description of a 232nd anniversary celebration and reenactment in April 2007 of the attack on Danbury. At the conclusion of the description, Hunt stated, "The festivities in Carmel [New York] implied an American victory, but in fact, the NY militia had not reached Danbury in time to prevent the British from destroying military provisions, torching the town, and fatally wounding Brigadier General David Wooster. The burning of Danbury, has, nevertheless, not harmed Sybil Ludington's reputation over the years."

My immediate reaction to her statement was, "Of course it did not harm Sybil Ludington's reputation over the years. Why would it?" Was she saying that an American loss should lessen the importance of Sybil's call to arms? I was also reminded of the statement made in the blog I had read as to whether the ride was actually an "important" American event of the war. Did the fact that "the NY militia had not reached Danbury in time to prevent the British from destroying military provisions, torching the town, and fatally wounding Brigadier General David Wooster" lessen the importance of Sybil's ride? The blog tells us that "Lamb didn't try to claim that the ride 'turned out to be important.'"

As I continue to apply my lens of the last twenty years, my continued belief in Sybil as a hero is renewed. In modern terms, the Colonel and his men were first responders. An alarm was sent out to warn that the British were attacking Connecticut, and stories, such as the one of young boys being hunted down and killed, were rampant. Innocent citizens were in danger of losing their homes and lives. Help was needed by all able-bodied Americans to come to the aid of their fellow Patriots. In the aftermath of the battle that ensued, the report by the committee appointed by the Connecticut General Assembly in May 1777 played over and over in my mind:

> *A committee appointed by the Connecticut General Assembly in May 1777 recorded the losses of 19 dwelling houses, the meetinghouse of the New Danbury Society, and 22 stores and barns, with all of their houses consumed. Howe reported British casualties as "One drummer and fife, and 23 rank and file killed; 3 field officers, 6 captains, 3 subalterns, 9 sergeants, 92 rank and file wounded; 1 drummer and fifer and 27 rank and file missing. Royal artillery: 2 additional killed, 3 matrosses and 1 wheeler wounded, and 1 matross missing."*
>
> *"Return of the rebels killed and wounded" were listed: "Killed: General Wooster; Colonel Gould; Colonel Lamb, of the artillery; Colonel Henman; Dr. Atwater, a man of considerable influence; Captain Cooe; Lieutenant Thompson; 100 privates; Wounded: Colonel Whiting; Captain Benjamin; Lieutenant Cooe; 250 privates. Taken: fifty privates, including several committeemen."*

Lamb tells us, "The families, suddenly, abandoning their homes, took such valuables as they could carry, but the greater portion of their household goods were left to the mercy of the foe. The church was packed to the gallery in barrels and several barns and depositories were filled to the roof; these were rolled into the street in a pile and the torch applied."[110]

I wondered about how many casualties it would take to make a battle "important." Exactly how many lives destroyed, dwellings burned and body bags accrued does it take to make a battle "significant"? And is a hero less of a hero if her side doesn't "win"? Hunt reassured me in our phone conversation that she was well aware of the importance of the battle and the losses that were incurred after the ride. She also reminded me that her article was not about whether the ride took place but about Sybil herself and how she has been viewed through the years.

Hunt tells us, "Sybil's ride embraces the mythical meanings and values expressed in the country's founding. As an individual she [Sybil] represents America's persistent need to find and create heroes who embody prevalent attitudes and beliefs." Hunt says she will "explore how Sybil was transformed into an American heroine, how her ride came to be considered a consequential part of the nation's foundational moment, and how her significance has been by turns heralded and challenged."

Hunt correctly credits Martha Lamb as authoring the first known written mention of Sybil's ride, not knowing at the time it was actually written in part by Charles H. Ludington, and notes that Lamb stated in her research that she had consulted a wide variety of primary sources gathered from private individuals, historians and libraries, including correspondence, "old sermons, records of trials, wills, genealogical manuscripts, documents and pamphlets." Hunt continues to say, "Given proof that she communicated with Ludington relatives it seems likely that her knowledge of Sybil's ride began there." Hunt mentions a letter in Lamb's files at the New-York Historical Society.

After checking with Hunt's footnotes, I returned to Lamb's files at the New-York Historical Society in New York City and found a letter written by "E.A. Smith" referring to a letter by "Mrs. Luddington" in box 6, folder 9. While I was surprised that I had missed the letter on an earlier trip there in 2012, I was elated to know of its existence. I hoped the letter could verify Lamb's source and pinpoint the origin of the Sybil Ludington "family legend"; however, the letter did not offer much.

Dear Friend,

I have just received a lovely note from Mrs. Ludington inclosing the five dollars. I have acknowledged the receipt of it and told her that as I was leaving so soon as I had told you about it and that you felt sensible the kindness of your [?] friends. The album is not returned. If not before I will give it to Mrs. Brown on Saturday. I'm awful hectic.
Loving,

E.A. Smith.

While I do concur that "it seems likely that Lamb's knowledge of Sybil's ride began there," I was not so sure it ended there. Where were the "wide variety of primary sources gathered from private individuals, historians, and libraries, including correspondence, 'old sermons, records of trials, wills, genealogical manuscripts, documents and pamphlets'" that Lamb referred to? Did they not exist? Or had we just not located them yet? Was she referring to the documentation collected by Lewis Patrick and Charles H. Ludington, such as Mrs. Comfort's recollections? My third and fourth trip to the New-York Historical Society gave me those answers.

In her article, Hunt continues to point out that mention of Sybil's ride by Lamb and Johnson was "singular" and notes the peculiarity that a bevy of authors and historians made no mention of Sybil's ride. Putnam County historians William J. Blake (1849); William Pelletreau (1888); Elizabeth Ellet's *Domestic History of the American Revolution* (1848–50); *Noble Deeds of American Women* (1851); *Daughters of America* (1882); and the *Romance of the Revolution* (1870) made no mention of Sybil. I failed to find that surprising. Most of these authors and books date from before Lamb's mention of the ride in 1880 or shortly after. They didn't write about it because they didn't know about it, not because they ignored it or didn't believe it happened. Ironically, Charles Ludington was in contact with some of these authors, and information on Sybil and the Ludingtons came directly from him, as evidenced in letters found in file #2 of MS 2692 Box 1. As for there being no mention of the ride in Sybil's lifetime or even by Sybil herself in her pension letters, it is simply that the importance of the ride was not realized until years later. In that, she joins many great artists, writers, minorities and women whose deeds or talents were not appreciated until years after their deaths. Even Sybil herself was likely not aware of the importance of her ride. Women were not allowed to be soldiers in Sybil's lifetime, and many of their brave acts were downplayed or went unnoticed.

Later, Hunt discusses the Sybil Ludington who was first introduced by Eric Berry, a pen name for Allena Champlin Best. In *Sybil Ludington's Ride*, Berry combines fact with fiction as she writes a tale for teens telling of Sybil's daring ride and her horse named Star. Some of these "fictional attributes" have come back to haunt Sybil as debunkers point out that these are fictional and not documented facts. Berry's book is, in fact, largely a work of fiction written to shed light on a real historical figure and event. Again here, I must caution readers to not be confused with later "facts" about Sybil's ride. While there may be fictionalized versions of her ride and possible later embellishments, the original telling of her ride came from her brother's son, a grandson of Colonel Henry Ludington's who gathered it from immediate family and Sybil herself.

Although the Enoch Crosby Chapter of the DAR was the proud recipient of Anna Hyatt Huntington's statue on Lake Gleneida and was largely responsible for her early recognition, Hunt tells us that Sybil's journey took a surprising detour in 1996 when the DAR denied the Enoch Crosby Chapter's application to mark Sybil's grave in Patterson, New York, recognizing Sybil as a National Patriot. The apparent reason was that the chapter "did not provide conclusive evidence of Sybil Ludington's Revolutionary War service, even though for decades the DAR's championing of the Revolutionary War's young heroine had suggested that she was an established DAR patriot." In my conversation with Paula Hunt on June 7, 2018, she confirmed her conversation with a member of the Enoch Crosby chapter and said she read letters from their files that explained the position of the National Society of the DAR. Although they supported Sybil as a daughter of a Revolutionary War Patriot, they did not believe they had enough evidence to meet their strict protocol for deeming Sybil a National Patriot. The first mention of the ride at the time was 1907. Today, there are family letters dating as far back as 1854 and sources for the reported stories that will hopefully shed new light on Sybil's life and ride.

In a 2006–7 museum exhibition, "Myth or Truth? Stories We've Heard about Early America," still accessible in January 2019 at www.dar.org/national-society/media-center/news-releases/dar-museum-exhibition-explores-early-american-myths, the DAR addressed Sybil's ride. Literature that accompanied the exhibition noted, "What we think: It's a great story, but there is no way to know whether or not it is true." Hunt also tells us that in a phone conversation with a DAR representative, she was told that a book about Sybil (*Women of the American Revolution*, by Mollie Somerville, published by the National Society Daughters of the American Revolution) was removed from a shelf in its bookstore. This information has prompted several articles and blogs that have repeated this information as a confirmation that the ride likely did not take place.[111]

Although Jennifer Pollack, regent (2016–19) for the Enoch Crosby Chapter of the National Society of the DAR, and her fellow members are committed to finding more documentation to deem Sybil a National Patriot, the National Society Daughters of the American Revolution seems to hold tight to its 2006 statement about Sybil and her famous ride:

Many people grew up believing that Betsy Ross was the designer of the first American flag or hearing tales of Sybil Ludington's heroic ride through the night to warn of the British coming. While no evidence has been found that proves the authenticity of those stories, it is just as intriguing to think about how such stories originate and to understand that tales like these are embraced as part of American history along with the facts of our founding fathers.[112]

A stunning example of the DAR's recognition of Sybil as a Revolutionary War hero is in its inclusion of Sybil in the first commemorative medal collection ever issued by the Daughters of the American Revolution. The series consists of thirty-six commemorative medals as a comprehensive medalic tribute to "The Great Women of the American Revolution." The collection was printed by the Franklin Mint at the rate of one medal per month from 1974 through 1977.[113] Sybil Ludington's medal is #20. On February 4, 2018, I purchased one of these fine, 45mm pewter medals with an antique finish on eBay for the amazing price of $12.30. One side of the coin bears a depiction of Sybil on horseback, with an unidentified male colonist waving as she passed. The reverse side bears the inscription "Great Women of the American Revolution"; the DAR insignia; and the following:

Sybil Ludington
She volunteered to ride alone
through the New York countryside
to muster her father's regiment.
Her mission was crucial to
the patriot victory
at Danbury

Unfortunately, as Hunt reminded us at the beginning of her article, *there was no Patriot victory in Danbury*, and once again, as was true with the back of the U.S. postage stamp in her honor, Sybil's history is marred by an error.

Hunt also reminds us that in its Washington, D.C. headquarters, the DAR continued to display a small replica of Sybil's statue and a large painting of Huntington sculpting it, but now the two works ostensibly celebrate Huntington as a renowned member of the DAR, not her subject. Since Hunt's article was published in 2015, I pulled up the DAR website to see if a replica of the Huntington statue and a painting of Anna Hyatt Huntington were still being displayed. They were, in the National Society of

DAR medal.

the Children of the American Revolution (NSCAR) Museum's Washington, D.C. headquarters, in an exhibit called "Freedom Thunder 2016–2017," on loan from the DAR. Below the painting, also prominently displayed, were copies of three of my own books on Sybil Ludington: *Sybil Ludington: The Call to Arms*; *Hauntings of the Hudson River Valley*; and *Sybil Ludington: Discovering the Life of a Revolutionary War Hero*,[114] all of which offer detailed accounts of Sybil's ride. The NSCAR exhibit read, "Kids During the Revolution— Sixteen-year old Sybil Ludington rode all through the night—even longer than Paul Revere—to let patriots know of the British attacking Danbury, Connecticut. Sybil was a child patriot of the American Revolution."[115] For a photo with the books, see the NSCAR website, nscar.org/NSCAR/aboutCAR/Headquarters.aspx. Click on "National Programs," then "2016–2017 Museum Tour—PDF Format," Slide 14.

The exhibit makes no mention of Anna Hyatt Huntington and is clearly a tribute to Sybil as a "child patriot." The NSCAR must be credited for its recognition of our American youth; however, in Sybil's case, she was sixteen at the time of her ride, legally a child today but no longer a "child" in her time. In the time and place in which she lived, Sybil was a grown woman. Her mother, Abigail, was married at fourteen and gave birth to Sybil at fifteen.

As her article continues, Hunt goes on to tell us that through it all, Sybil has somehow managed to hold her place on her pedestal in Putnam County. Hunt says, "Sybil went on to make a decided impression on twentieth-century Putnam and Dutchess County residents." She mentions, of course, the

NSCAR Museum exhibit. *Courtesy of the National Society of the Children of the American Revolution Museum.*

statue, as well as the stamp, road markers and various honors conferred on Sybil, and quotes speeches praising Sybil for her bravery and service to her country. She cites Putnam County executive MaryEllen Odell's comment about Sybil in her state-of-the-year address: "Putnam, from the days of Sybil Ludington, has always stood for the principles of what has made our country great: tolerance and respect, freedom and values." I was actually surprised to see that Hunt also quotes an article about one of my lectures, where I referred to Sybil as "exactly what Americans are made of."

Hunt lavishly explains "sweeping social changes" in American history through the many years since Sybil's ride and offers a clear understanding of why Americans, Putnam residents in particular, hold on to a belief in Sybil. In fact, there was a resurgence of an appreciation for the Revolutionary War in the 1800s, about the time that Martha Lamb wrote about Sybil, and the rise in women's organizations and movements. Perhaps a resurgence for Sybil's rights will also be energized by the 2018 #METOO movement for women's rights and enable Sybil sympathizers to have Sybil recognized as a National Patriot, especially in view of the new information discovered at the New-York Historical Society.

The real point of Hunt's article is summarized in the last paragraph: "In the end, Sybil Ludington has embodied the possibilities—the courage, individuality, loyalty—that Americans of different genders, generations, and political persuasions have considered to be the highest aspirations for themselves and for their country. The story of the lone, teenage girl riding for freedom, it seems, is simply just too good not to be believed."[116]

Chapter 9

SYBIL LIVES ON

Reverence and respect for Sybil Ludington has far from diminished despite a belief by some that the ride never took place. On July 19, 2012, I was honored to attend and help host a Ludington family reunion. I had already been to one in New Haven, Connecticut, and two in Ludington, Michigan. This one, in 2012, was in Sybil's own backyard—Putnam (formerly Dutchess) County. The family was greeted with open arms and invited by the County Historian's Office, which hosted a "Family Research Day" and co-hosted a luncheon with the County Executive's Office in the family's honor. The event was held at the Cornerstone Memorial Park and Conference Center, located on Route 52 in Carmel, New York, along the possible route Sybil traveled the night of her ride. A highlight of the lunch was a presentation of a proclamation to the family by MaryEllen Odell, Putnam County executive, one of Sybil's most ardent admirers and supporters. The proclamation said it all:

> *Sybil Ludington Day & Sybil Appreciation Week*
> *WHEREAS, the year 2012 marks the Bicentennial Year of the formation of Putnam County; and*
> *WHEREAS, Sybil Ludington Ogden is a recognized female hero of the American Revolution who at the young age of sixteen rode for freedom on April 26, 1777, to alert her father's, Colonel Henry Ludington's, troops that the British were burning Danbury, Connecticut; and*

WHEREAS, as Americans who revel in our freedom, we must see to it that all heroic deeds of the women and men and children of our beloved Country and County never be forgotten; and

WHEREAS Thursday, July 19, 2012, the Ludington family, descendants of Sybil Ludington Ogden, will formally gather to celebrate the County's Bicentennial Year; and

WHEREAS, Sybil Ludington Day and Sybil Ludington Appreciation Week promotes the recognition of all heroic deeds of the women, men and children of our beloved Country and County, now therefore be it

RESOLVED, that Putnam County Executive MaryEllen Odell and the Putnam County Legislature on behalf of all the citizens of Putnam County, proclaim Thursday, July 19, 2012 to be observed as Sybil Ludington Day and the week of July 15–July 21, 2012 as Sybil Ludington Appreciation Week in Putnam County. All citizens are encouraged to commemorate the day and week with the appropriate observances and by the remembrance of Sybil Ludington and all those who contributed by acts of bravery to America's quest for independence and freedom for all.

On April 28, 2012, the Kent Historical Society invited members of the community to join in celebrating a reenactment of Sybil's ride. The event, organized by Kent councilman John Greene, featured a trolley to take visitors on portions of the famous route. Sixteen-year-old Marki-Lynne Sullivan portrayed Sybil as she rode through the event on horseback.[117] The reenactment is one of many in recent years; Ms. Sullivan joins a long list of young female equestrians who have ridden in Sybil's name. The Kent Historical Society has also long been an advocate of the Ludingtons and maintains the mill site formerly owned by Colonel Ludington and his family. In my 2018 interview with President Clark Darling, he confirmed the society's commitment to raise funds for the rebuilding of the mill destroyed by fire in 1972 so that local students and future residents of Putnam may see what the mill may have looked like in Sybil's time.

Celebrations held in the spirit of our popular culture have also not forgotten Sybil over the years. On or about April 26 of each year, the Annual Sybil Ludington Historical Run is held in Carmel, New York. The event is composed of two races: a 50K race and a two-person relay. Runners essentially run along the route that Sybil may have taken on the night of her famous ride, where they are greeted by hundreds of supporters. Last year marked the thirty-eight-year celebration of the ride.[118]

The Putnam County Veterans Museum was granted a five-year provisional charter "from the Board of Regents for and on behalf of the Education Department for the State of New York at their meeting of March 11, 2014. The purpose for which said corporation [was] formed: a) is to document the lives and experiences of men and women who served our country; and, b) to identify, collect, preserve, exhibit and make available for research artifacts and instructional records for use of historians, educators, and the general public." Sybil and her ride of April 26, 1777, are proudly displayed among the artifacts and records of the many men and women who served in the various wars that followed the American Revolution. The museum is located in the Putnam County Veteran's Memorial Park on Gipsy Trail Road in Carmel, New York.

A two-day encampment and reenactment in April 2007—cosponsored by the Reed Public Library in Carmel, the Living History Guild, Putnam County Historical Societies, Greater Mahopac-Carmel Chamber of Commerce, Putnam Visitors Bureau, Drew Methodist Church and the New York Department of Environmental Protection—brought visitors from all over the county to honor Sybil and her father.[119]

Putnam County Veterans Museum.

The year 2017 also brought a resurgence of pride for Sybil Ludington as it marked the 240th celebration of her famous ride and the Battle of Ridgefield. In Carmel, fans gathered on April 27 to hear speeches of praise for the young heroine. Revolutionary War reenactors relived the event, as "Colonel Ludington" walked about in full regalia, portrayed by historian Larry Maxwell, and "Sybil Ludington," played by Kailie Nolan of East Durham, rode along the shores of Lake Gleneida on horseback by Sybil's statue to mingle with dozens of faithful Sybil fans and schoolchildren who arrived on school buses to witness the event.

Twenty miles east of this event, citizens of Ridgefield, Connecticut, featured a colonial encampment, walking tours, several lectures at the famous Keeler Tavern and Museum with speakers such as myself and a parade down Main Street with a "Sybil Ludington" of their own on horseback to oversee the "skirmishes" between British and colonial troops dressed in authentic period uniforms, firing off cannons and musket shots, to the delight of hundreds of onlookers who lined the street. The parade was followed by an evening black-tie affair to celebrate the anniversary of the Battle of Ridgefield. The event was organized by Jerusalem 49 Masonic Lodge and the 1777 Wooster Sons of Liberty Foundation.[120]

Perhaps one of the most interesting popular culture statements bestowed on Sybil is the Sybil Ludington Women's Freedom Award, given by the National Rifle Association in her name "to honor her accomplishment and the accomplishments of modern-day heroines." Recipients date back to 1995 and include Sarah Palin, the ninth governor of Alaska from 2006 to 2009 and former vice-presidential Republican nominee in 2008, who received the award in 2010. In his *NRA: An American Legend*, Jefferey L. Rodegen says the award was established "so that the National Rifle Association of America could express its profound appreciation and gratitude to the many women who have selflessly advanced the purposes and objectives of the Association." Recipients are presented with a bronze sculpture by Jane Tucker entitled *Freedom*.[121]

Chapter 10

CLOSING COMMENTS

D id Sybil Ludington make a dangerous and important ride on the night of April 26, 1777, to summon her father's troops? While documentation of some facts of this case are not clear, other facts are irrefutable: General Tryon of the British army did invade Connecticut with two thousand troops at the end of April 1777, according to documented military reports; Colonel Ludington, according to sworn depositions by his troops, did take part in the American fight to suppress the British; and, according to records obtained from Colonel Howe's official report and records from a committee appointed by the Connecticut General Assembly in May 1777, a considerable loss of property and lives was sustained in Connecticut in the raid by General Tryon and British troops during the period in question.

So, what do *I* think? Did the Colonel's daughter risk her life on the evening of April 26, 1777, to alert his troops that they were needed to help repel the British in Danbury, Connecticut? I would like to say here that I have recordings from surveillance cameras along her route, but there were of course no video cams in 1777. There were also no roving reporters to capture events of the times. As for handwritten records of daily events such as diaries and journals by the Colonel's militia, they were rarely written by members of the militia nor their families, who were generally farmers, merchants and innkeepers. Many of them were skilled but illiterate. Records of their births and marriages were, if at all, only recorded on a page in the family Bible. There was no online service to help them explore their genealogy, let alone their daily and historic events, and there were no e-mails, Twitters or texts. An act of heroism, such as a ride into the night to muster men against an enemy, especially by a young woman, would only be remembered and passed down through the family or other primary witnesses orally or in letters. Today, we have some of those precious documents. Many of the most important facts about our early American history rely totally on the recollections of important events by family members, such as the time Sybil saved her famous father's life with her sister Rebecca. There simply was no one else to witness it and record it. Thankfully, in some cases, there are documents such as depositions to obtain pensions for time served in the military. One such deposition was submitted by Jonathan Carley, a neighbor of the Ludingtons and member of one of Colonel Ludington's regiments. In a letter for the purpose of obtaining a pension, Carley stated that he

> *was born in 1757, in Wilton, Connecticut. While a resident of South East Town, Dutchess County, New York, Jonathan Carley enlisted on March 20, 1775, served six months in Captain Barnum's company, Colonel Field's New York regiment, enlisted in the spring of 1776, served six months in Captain Barnum's company, Colonel field's regiment, and was in the battle of White Plains where he had nineteen ball holes shot through his body, one in his breast, one in his right shoulder which broke his bone, three flesh wounds in his left arm and one in his hip as result of which he was cripple. He enlisted in February 1777, in Captain Luddington's company of minute men, Colonel Luddington's New York regiment for nine months, went with the regiment on the line but the fatigue was too much for him by reasons of his wounds so he was placed in a hospital where he remained about six months, then carried home and was ill for a long time. He enlisted in September 1781, served five months as sergeant in Colonel Luddington's regiment.*[122]

The letter and application offered something very significant: a signed deposition by Sybil herself supporting the application of Jonathan Carley, who served in the Colonel's regiment. The letter was signed by the Honorable Gilbert Cane, Justice, and reads as follows:

> *State of New York*
> *Otsego County, NY*
> *Sibil Ogden of the Town of Unadilla in the County of Otsego—aged Seventy-Three years, being duly sworn says that she is the daughter of Col.*

State of New York
Otsego County

Sibel Ogden of the Town of Unadilla in the Coun =ty of Otsego – aged Twenty three years – being duly Sworn says – That she is a daughter of Col. Henry Ludington (deceased) formerly of the County of Dutchess – That she knew Jonathan Carley who now resides in the Town of Sidney in the County of Delaware during the War of the Revolution – That her Father during the War resided in Freder =ick's Town in the County of Dutchess and commanded a Regiment of Mili =tia – that he also commanded a Corn or Regiment of Men entitled as "Nine months men" – but cannot say in what year this one was raised – That her Father was frequently and almost constantly engaged in active service from the commencement to the close of the War – near what was then called "the lines" and elsewhere as occasion occurred in repressing the incursions of the British and Tories &c. That during the War the said Carley was often at her Fathers House – that she has no distinct recollection of any particular services rendered by him but from conversation with said Carley and from various facts and circumstances related by him with which this deponent was acquainted at the time they occurred she believes he must have served occasionally as a soldier in her Fathers Regiment That detachments from said Regiment were almost constantly kept upon the alert to counteract the designs and incursions of the Tories and British and believed that said Carley was occasionally at least engaged in such detached services –

Sworn this 1st February
1834 Before me –
Gilbert Coun Justice

Sibel Ogden

Pension Application File #S23152, Jonathan Carley.

Henry Ludington (deceased) formerly of the County of Dutchess—that she knew Jonathan Carley who now resides in the town of Sydney in the County of Delaware—during the War of the Revolution—that her father during the war resided in Frederick's Town in the County of Dutchess and commanded a regiment of militia—that he also commanded a core or regiment of men entitled as "Nine Months Men"—but cannot say in what year this core was raised—that her father was most frequently and constantly engaged in active service from the commencement to the close of the war—near what was then called "the lines" and elsewhere as occasion occurred in repressing the incursions of the British and Tories.

That during the war—the said Carley was often at her father's house—that she has no distinct recollection of any particular services rendered by him but from conversation with said Carley and from various facts and circumstances by him with which this deponent was acquainted at the time they occurred she believed he must have served occasionally—as a soldier in her father's Regiment—that detachments from said regiment were almost constantly kept upon the alert to counteract the designs and incursions of the Tories and British and believed that said Carley was occasionally at least engaged in such detailed services.

Signed

Sibel Ogden

Sworn this 1ˢᵗ February 1834 Before Me Gilbert Cane Justice

I certify that Sibil Ogden who has submitted and sworn to the above is known to me as a person of truth and veracity and is an accepted witness.

The Carley letter falls short of saying that Sybil herself was involved in calling out alarms, but let us not forget the way in which the actions of courageous women were viewed (or not viewed) at the time and the deposition of James Mead, who stated "he was frequently called out on alarm the first for the term of two weeks at the time Danbury was burnt by the British army in Captain Joel Mead's company, Col. Luddington's regiment."

We must also remember that on the night before Colonel Ludington left for Danbury with his troops, a messenger arrived on a rainy Sunday night at approximately 9:00 p.m. (weather reports of the time confirm rainy conditions). All of the Colonel's children were younger than Sybil.

The messenger was exhausted and unfamiliar with the area. The Colonel's militiamen were likely asleep early because it was April planting season. We must assume that Sybil knew the route she must take and was aware of her father's involvement in the war and his soldiers, like Carley, who frequented the house. The Colonel had to be home when his men arrived and was unable to make the ride himself. Who else would have been capable of calling out the alert to summon the men to the parade grounds on that night? No debunker or primary document I've read has mentioned any other possible rider.

In the case of Sybil Ludington, the first published mention of her ride came to us from Martha J. Lamb, a noted historian in 1880, only forty-one years after Sybil's death. We now know she received her information in 1878 from Charles Henry Ludington, Sybil's nephew, who wrote of the event as early as 1854. In the preface of her book, Lamb states, "I have done what I could to learn the truth. No one authority has been accepted and followed in any instance without further evidences; and where accounts have conflicted, I have sought and secured every book and document I could find relating to the subject, of which I could obtain knowledge, even if no more than one of my paragraphs was involved in an issue." I, too, have sought and secured every book and document I could find relating to the subject, and no one authority has been accepted and followed in any instance without further evidence or research. I also firmly believe there is more evidence to be found.

Lamb continued, "To the various New York families who have constantly and courteously given me access to private-libraries and valuable family manuscripts—more precious than diamonds—I cannot express too warmly my grateful acknowledgments."[123] Unfortunately, Lamb failed to document her valuable sources, thereby bringing into doubt the validity of Sybil's story. Today, her sources are clear, and I would like to express *my* grateful acknowledgements to the many people who diligently worked to preserve Sybil's story, in particular Charles Henry Ludington, Lavinia Ludington, Lewis S. Patrick and the various family members who contributed to the information now available at the New-York Historical Society's Research Center, as well as Jane Ross Ludington and Charles Townsend Ludington Jr. for donating their valuable family documents—more precious than diamonds.

Paula Hunt, in her essay, seems to feel that the reason for a belief in Sybil stems from a social need to create a hero. I believe Sybil simply *was* a hero. The question here is not why she rode, or why we want to believe she is a hero for riding, or even if her story was embellished; the question is whether she rode at all. If she did, and I see no reason to believe she didn't, she is indeed "a contributor to the cause," as the United States Postal Service suggests, and risked her life in doing so.

In short, all available facts indicate that on the night of April 26, 1777, sixteen-year-old Sybil Ludington rode to call out her father's troops to aid the citizens of Connecticut and risked her life because American lives and their property were in danger—and in at least one instance saved the life of an important American Patriot leader. In those respects, she should be recognized, without errors in her biography or an error of omission from the list of our many other national heroes, male and female, young and old, as an example of exactly what great Americans are made of.

Quick-Reference Chart

Fact	Source	Resources/Notes
Sybil Ludington's ride on April 26, 1777, and courageous attempt to save her father's life is documented in family recollections and correspondence dating back as early as 1854.	"The Ludington Family Papers," MS 2962, New-York Historical Society's Research Library. Collection donated by Jane Ludington in 2015.	New-York Historical Society's Research Library, 170 Central Park West, New York, NY 10024 (second floor)
Sybil's parents were both Luddingtons. Her father's father and her mother's father were brothers. Sybil's parents were first cousins.	Johnson, *Colonel Henry Ludington*.	Putnam County Historian's Office, Brewster, NY.
Henry was among the first Luddingtons to drop the second *d* in his name. The name also appears in documents as "Ludenton."	Ludington and Forest, *Ludington-Saltus Records*, 152.	New-York Historical Society's Research Library, 170 Central Park West, New York, NY 10024 (second floor).
In 1761, Sybil arrived with her parents in Fredericksburgh at Lot Number 6 of the Philipse Patent in New York State, where Henry operated a successful gristmill. Sybil lived with her parents in their house until her marriage in 1784.	Pelletreau, *History of Putnam County*. Family sketch written to William Pelletreau in 1886.	Available in most Putnam County libraries. Letter available at New-York Historical Society's Research Library.

FACT	SOURCE	RESOURCES/NOTES
The Ludingtons raised twelve children in Fredericksburgh: Sybil, born April 5, 1761; Rebecca, born 1763; Mary, born 1765; Archibald, born 1767; Henry, born 1769; Derick, born 1771; Tertullus, born 1773; Abigail, born 1776; Anna, born 1778; Frederick, born 1782; Sophia, born 1784; Lewis, born June 1786.	See ledger in New-York Historical Society's Research Library, 170 Central Park West, New York, NY 10024 (second floor). Box 1, "The Ludington Family Papers," MS 2962.	The names of the Ludington children were recorded in a ledger kept by the Colonel. See Johnson, *Colonel Henry Ludington*, 45.
Henry Ludington served his king as a captain of the Fifth Company of the Second Battalion of the Fredericksburgh Regiment of Militia in Dutchess County. By 1776, however, he had become a staunch revolutionary, prompting General Howe, the British commander, to offer a reward of 300 English guineas for Ludington "dead or alive." A letter from his grandson in 1854 quoted the reward as "several hundred pounds."	See letter of 1854 to Henry Deming, Esq., from Charles H. Ludington, the Colonel's grandson.	New-York Historical Society's Research Library, 170 Central Park West, New York, NY 10024 (second floor).
The first *public* mention of Sybil's ride was in 1880 by Martha J. Lamb.	Lamb, *History of the City of New York*, 159–60.	New-York Historical Society Library.
Sybil (also spelled "Sibbell," "Sibyl," "Sibel" and "Sebal") was referred to as her father's "most vigilant and watchful companion.…Her constant care and thoughtfulness, combined with fortuitous circumstances, prevented the fruition of many an intrigue against his life and capture."	Patrick, "Secret Service of the American Revolution," 271–72.	Generally available in libraries along the Connecticut border in Westchester and Putnam Counties. A copy may be found in the Danbury Public Library.

Fact	Source	Resources/Notes
Danbury, Connecticut, was raided and burned on April 27, 1777, by William Tryon, royal governor of New York, major general of Loyalist Provincials and commander of the Danbury expedition. His mission was to destroy the revolutionaries' supplies reported to be stored there. Tryon's troops from twenty transports and six war vessels embarked at Compo Point near Norwalk at approximately 4:00 p.m. on April 25. By Sunday, April 28, many people had been killed or wounded. Nineteen dwelling houses, the meetinghouse of the New Danbury Society and twenty-two stores and barns with all their contents were torched.	Jones, *History of New York.* Bailey, *History of Danbury.* Hollister, *History of Connecticut*, 296–308.	Danbury Public Library.
Included in the materials destroyed: "4,000 barrels of beef and pork; 100 large tierces of biscuits; 89 barrels of rice; 120 puncheons of rum; several large stores of wheat, oats and Indian corn…30 pipes of wine; 100 hogsheads of sugar; 50 dittos of molasses; 20 casks of coffee; 15 large casks filled with medicine of all kinds." The revolutionary dead included General David Wooster. Benedict Arnold's horse was shot from under him.	Case, *Tryon's Raid*, 27. Also mentioned in Lamb, *History of the City of New York*, 159, but amounts vary.	Connecticut accounts of Tryon's raid are accessible in libraries and historic houses along Tryon's route: Westport, Weston, Redding, Bethel, Danbury, Ridgefield, Wilton and Norwalk.

FACT	SOURCE	RESOURCES/NOTES
Colonel Ludington was called on to muster his men and come to the aid of revolutionary troops en route to Danbury. Sybil rode forty miles through a rainy night to alert her father's troops, the Seventh Regiment Dutchess County Militia.	Johnson, *Colonel Henry Ludington*.	USMA Library. See also Dutchess County Historical Society in Poughkeepsie, New York.
Sybil was aware of the dangers she would face going out alone that night, including army deserters, "Cowboys," "Skinners" and Royalists. Her ride through the New York countryside resulted in the Colonel's being able to get to Ridgefield to aid in the battle that helped drive Tryon back to his ships.	Lamb, *History of the City of New York*, 159–60. Patrick, "Secret Service of the American Revolution," 271–72.	Lamb's book can be found in New-York Historical Society Library. Patrick's article in the *Connecticut Magazine* can be found in the Danbury Public Library.
Sybil's route has been marked throughout areas of Putnam County since 1934.	Torrey, "Signs to Mark Historic Ride."	Road markers today still denote Sybil's route, Colonel Ludington's parade grounds, the former Ludington home site and the Colonel's route to Connecticut. *Herald Tribune* article may be found in files in the Putnam County Historian's Office in Brewster, New York. See also: Dutchess County Historical Society in Poughkeepsie, New York. Map of Sybil's ride showing historic markers and the location of the Ludington Mill is available at the Putnam County Historian's Office.
The Colonel's participation in the Danbury affair is documented in depositions of several of his troops.	Darley, *Call to Arms*.	See pension records quoted in this book.

FACT	SOURCE	RESOURCES/NOTES
In 1907, Sybil's ride was mentioned in a memoir by Willis Fletcher Johnson commissioned by family members. Louis S. Patrick wrote an account of the ride in *Connecticut Magazine* in 1907. This is likely the same person whom Willis Fletcher Johnson credited as Lewis S. Patrick in his memoirs of the Colonel. "Both" men were known as thorough researchers of colonial American history. Charles Ludington was also engaged in eliciting information from the family. While Willis Fletcher Johnson is said to be responsible for helping Sybil receive credit for her ride, Johnson clearly credits Patrick and Charles Ludington for "the collection of a large share of the data upon which this memoir of his ancestor is founded." Inaccuracies by Johnson and others have made it difficult for later researchers to investigate Sybil's life beyond her ride. The most common confusion was with her husband's first name.	Johnson, *Colonel Henry Ludington*, 219. Patrick, "Secret Service of the American Revolution," 273. Pelletreau, *History of Putnam County*.	USMA Library and the Kent Historical Society in Kent, New York. Pelletreau's *History of Putnam County* available at all Putnam County libraries.
Researchers had long hoped that some mention of the ride before 1907 could be found in military records or family letters or diaries. We now know that the first public mention was by Martha J. Lamb in 1880 and that she received her information from Charles Ludington in 1778.	"Ludington Family Papers," MS 2962, New-York Historical Society's Research Library. Collection donated by Jane Ludington in 2015.	New-York Historical Society's Research Library, 170 Central Park West, New York, NY 10024 (second floor).

Fact	Source	Resources/Notes
Sybil and Edmond Ogden were married on October 24, 1784, in Patterson, New York. In a letter to the War Department, Sybil's sister Mary Gilbert of Poughkeepsie said she witnessed the wedding of the couple by Reverend Ebenezer Coles, Baptist clergyman in Patterson, Dutchess (now Putnam) County. Edmond was twenty-nine years old and Sybil was twenty-three.	Letter from Mrs. Gilbert in the National Archives (Pension Files R 7777), "Ogden, Edmond; Sebal." Jacobus, *History and Genealogy*, 239.	Pension files available at National Archives and Records Administration, Washington, D.C., 20408. See most Connecticut libraries for Jacobus, *History and Genealogy*.
Sybil's husband was incorrectly identified as Henry Ogden in Pelletreau's *History of Putnam County* in 1886. His source of information was Charles Ludington, the Colonel's grandson.	Pelletreau, *History of Putnam County*. "Ludington Family Papers," MS 2962, New-York Historical Society's Research Library. Collection donated by Jane Ludington in 2015.	Pelletreau's *History* is generally available in Putnam County libraries. Letters available at New-York Historical Society's Research Library.
In the Ludington memoirs by Johnson, Edmond was listed as "Edward (the name elsewhere given as Edmund or Henry)" and later in the same book as "Henry (elsewhere called Edward or Edmund")."	Johnson, *Colonel Henry Ludington*.	Putnam County Historian's Office.
J.H. Beers also mistakenly identified Henry as Sybil's husband in 1897.	Beers, *Commemorative Biographical Record*, 978.	New York and New York State Historical Association Library, Cooperstown, NY.
A commonly repeated comment about Sybil's later life states that she married Edmond Ogden, "her childhood sweetheart." This first appeared in 1949. Edmond's military record, however, clearly shows him as having been a resident of Connecticut when he entered the service in 1776.	Ephlin, "Girl Who Outrode Paul Revere."	See vertical file in Mahopac Public Library.

Fact	Source	Resources/Notes
Sybil's husband was born in Connecticut and was living there at the time of her ride. His parents, Humphrey and Hannah Ogden, moved to "Fredericksborough" in 1783—one year before Sybil and Edmond were married. Although there is no deed on record for the purchase of land in "Fredericksborough" for Humphrey Ogden Sr., there is a deed for the sale of land on June 7, 1887, "between Humphry Ogden and Hannah his wife and Humphrey Ogden Junior all of Fredericksborough Precinct in Dutchess County and State of New York of the one part and John Townsend of Oyster Bay in Queens County and State aforesaid of the other part." Several deeds listed for Humphrey Jr. and both "Humphrey Ogden Jr. of Fredericksburg" and "his father" are discussed by Pelletreau in a New York land transaction with John Townsend (p. 650).	Jacobus, *History and Genealogy*, 239. *Index to Deeds—Dutchess County, N.Y.* Grantees 1757–1785 Humphrey Ogden Jr., Liber 9, p. 122. Grantor: William B. Alger. Dutchess County, 1785, Humphrey Ogden Jr. Liber 9, p. 126. See also Pelletreau, *History of Putnam County*, 639, 650, 657.	Maps and deeds located in the county clerk's office in Poughkeepsie, NY.
There is also evidence that both Edmond and his father served in the Third Regiment of the New York Militia after their arrival in New York.	Roberts, *New York in the Revolution*, 241–42. This edition contains a special notation as follows: "These records were discovered arranged and classified in 1895, 1896, 1897, and 1898."	New-York Historical Society Library.

Fact	Source	Resources/Notes
At the time of Sybil's ride, her future husband, Sergeant Edmond Ogden, had just returned from a one-year tour of duty under Captain Albert Chapman and Colonel Elmore. He had enlisted at Weston, Fairfield County, in April 1776 and served until April 18, 1777 (eight days before Sybil's famous ride). He served at German Flats, Fort Dayton and Fort Stanwix. In 1778, he served an additional six to eight months in the navy. He is recorded as having served at sea on board the "Bony Richard" (*Bonhomme Richard*) and other vessels. Sybil's pension claim of 1837 was made when she was seventy-six years old. (Pensions "For Certain Widows" were granted by an act of Congress in July 1836.) Sybil signed a letter of deposition for a pension application in September 1838. She died on February 26, 1839. Sybil's claim was denied because she could not produce her marriage certificate. Sybil signed a letter of deposition stating she married Edmond on October 24, 1764, but she did not attend the court hearing, "by reason of her age, bodily infirmities, and general disability." A copy of the claim rejection appears in this book.	Record of Service of Connecticut Men in the War of the Revolution. General Assembly, Hartford, 1889. Pension File #R 7777 Conn. Navy "Ogden, Edmond; Sebal." A summary of these records also appears in Jacobus, *History and Genealogy*. See also a letter a letter from Sybil's granddaughter seeking information regarding proof of Sybil's marriage.	A copy of the files is in the National Archives in New York City, 1 Varick Street, twelfth floor. Northeastern Region M804. See Fold3.

Fact	Source	Resources/Notes
Edmond Ogden's parents were Hannah Bennett and Humphrey Ogden of Westport, Connecticut. They married at Westport, November 22, 1743. (Hannah was the daughter of Thomas Bennett.) They had eleven children: ANN—born 11/2/1744, baptized 11/25, married 4/7/1762 to John Coley MARY—born 4/3/1747, baptized 4/26, married 4/22/1770 to Nathan Sturges JOSEPH—born 3/1/1749, baptized 3/19, married 10/3/71 to Rachel Daniels HUMPHREY—born 2/21/1751, baptized 2/24 SARAH—born 1/24/1753, baptized 2/4, married 12/24/72 to Stephen Hurlbut EDMOND—born 2/12/1755, baptized 3/2, died in N.Y. State 9/16/99; married at Patterson, Putnam County, New York, 10/24/1784 (pension rec.), Sybil, who was living 1838 Unadilla, Otsego County, NY. EUNICE—born 12/28/1756, baptized 1/16/57, married 11/19/78 to Pinkney Beers NATHAN—baptized 1/15/1759, married 4/13/1780 to Hannah Goodsell HANNAH—baptized at Weston 7/27/1760 ELIZABETH—baptized 2/26/1763 RHODA—baptized 8/3/1766	Jacobus, *History and Genealogy*, 712–13. Fred Bowman and Thomas J. Lynch, *7000 Hudson-Mohawk Valley (NY) Vital Records 1808–1850*, 228. Bowman, *8000 More Vital Records*. Baily, *Early Connecticut Marriages*.	Searching through the IGA North America Family Series at the Yorktown Family History Center of the Church of Jesus Christ of Latter-day Saints, Route 134, Yorktown Heights, NY, I found the address of Edward Lanyon Woodyard, whose discovery of the Connecticut connection in the Edmond Ogden line was the key to finding new and important information about Sybil's life.

FACT	SOURCE	RESOURCES/NOTES
In 1935, through the untiring efforts of the Enoch Crosby Chapter of the DAR, the New York State Department of Education, the Division of Highways and the American Scenic and Historic Preservation Society, roadside markers were placed along the route that Sybil took on April 26, 1777.	*Putnam County Courier*, "Five Historic Roadside Markers."	Putnam County Historian's Office.
The 1935 road markers sparked several articles and new interest in Sybil Ludington.	*Putnam County Courier Trader*, "Revolutionary War Service."	New York State Historical Association Library, Cooperstown, NY.
Many articles following the 1949 piece in *Coronet* carry a standard paragraph about Sybil's life after her ride that was similar to this: "After her famous midnight ride, Sybil Ludington married Henry Ogden who became a Catskill lawyer and was Sybil's childhood sweetheart. They had four sons and two daughters and moved to Unadilla, New York. One of her sons. Major Edmund Ogden, became a distinguished national military figure in the mid-1800s." Anna Hyatt Huntington created a statue of Sybil Ludington dedicated in 1961.	Ephlin, "Girl Who Outrode Paul Revere," 50–52. Masters, "Anna Hyatt Huntington," C4. Articles that include similar paragraphs about Sybil are listed in the bibliography at the end of this book and are discussed at length in the text.	New York State Historical Association Library, Cooperstown, NY. The *Patent Trader* in Cross River, NY. Libraries throughout Putnam and Dutchess Counties have files on Sybil Ludington with photographs and clippings that may be photocopied by patrons.
In 1921, Reverend George Noble of Carmel, NY, wrote a poem in Sybil's honor. It did not attain the fame of Longfellow's poem about Paul Revere. Berton Braley, a famous poet, penned a poem in 1940 similar in style to Longfellow's poem.	Braley's poem was published in *New York Herald Tribune*'s *This Week Magazine*, April 14, 1940. *Poughkeepsie Journal*, April 28, 1975, includes a copy of Berton Braley's poem.	Mahopac Public Library Vertical File

Quick-Reference Chart

Fact	Source	Resources/Notes
Another poem by Marjorie Barstow Greenbie in 1963 was set to music and presented at the unveiling of a statue of Sybil in the gardens of the National Women's Party at 144 Constitution Avenue NE, Washington, D.C. The poem was later read into the *Congressional Record*. The song was made available by mail order on a ten-inch record. Much of the credit for Sybil's recognition as a hero is due to the efforts of the Enoch Crosby Chapter of the Daughters of the American Revolution, which has consistently fought for Sybil's right to have a place in America's history. An opera, poems, a statue and a postage stamp are among the honors accorded Sybil. Students who study her as part of New York State's curriculum on local history write dozens of reports and poems on Sybil annually. Unfortunately, many of the reports and poems by the children contain the same mistakes perpetuated for years by journalists and historians.	*Congressional Record*, Appendix A3169, May 20, 1963, includes copy of Greenbie poem. See bibliography for extensive list of articles on tributes paid to Sybil Ludington.	Copies of both Noble and Braley poems are in the "Sybil Ludington box" in Reed Library, Carmel, NY, and in various libraries throughout Putnam, Westchester and Dutchess Counties.

FACT	SOURCE	RESOURCES/NOTES
The DAR was instrumental in informing the public of Sybil's ride but included two errors in a magazine article published in 1949. Although it correctly identified Sybil's husband as Edmond, it incorrectly stated that Sybil had four sons and two daughters and that two of her sons became officers in the army—one of them E.A. Ogden. The Dutchess County Historical Society *Yearbook* for 1945 identified Sybil, also incorrectly, as the wife of a Catskill lawyer and mother of four sons and two daughters.	Ephlin, "Girl Who Outrode Paul Revere," 50–52. *Yearbook*, Dutchess County Historical Society, 81.	Dutchess Historical Society, Poughkeepsie, NY.
Although most articles claimed that she was the mother of six children, Sybil Ludington was the mother of only one child, Henry, who became a lawyer in Catskill and later moved to Unadilla. Henry fathered six children. The early mention of Henry as Sybil's husband confused researchers for years. Janet Wethy Foley was the lone researcher to provide correct information. Others writing about Sybil ignored her 1934 piece. There is no evidence of birth records, death records, census records or education records for any of Sybil's alleged children except Henry.	Foley, *Early Settlers of New York State*.	New-York Historical Society Library, New York.

FACT	SOURCE	RESOURCES/NOTES
Sybil and her husband are listed in a deed in Dutchess County for property formerly owned by her father. The deed is for the sale of property from Edmond Ogden of Fredericks Town and County of Dutchess and State of New York and Sybil, his wife, to Samuel, Augustus Barker of Fredericks Town, dated April 23, 1793.	Dutchess County clerk's office, Ogden-Barker Deed, Liber 12, p. 62.	
Sybil is listed in 1789 as a member of the congregation of the Presbyterian Church of Patterson-Pawling, New York.	Frost, "Chronological History of the Presbyterian Church of Patterson-Pawling."	Reverend Frost served at the Presbyterian Church of Pawling-Patterson for thirty years before becoming pastor in Saugerties, NY.
Edmond's name appears in an ad for the sale of land Colonel Ludington had acquired near Pawling. Johnson mentions trips to this property by Sybil and her sister Rebecca. It is likely that Sybil also visited Edmond on her trips and eventually settled there with him for the first few years of their marriage.	1790 census for Dutchess County, No. 45,266, Frederickstown (taken on Jan. 3, 1791).	Yorktown Family History Center, Church of Jesus Christ of Latter-day Saints, Yorktown Heights, NY.
Sybil Ludington can be found in the 1790 census living with her husband, one male child "seven or under" and one male "white" adult. In this same census, Ludington is spelled Ludenton.	Heads of Families at the First Census of the United States Taken in the Year 1790.	Yorktown Family History Center, Church of Jesus Christ of Latter-day Saints, Yorktown Heights, NY.

FACT	SOURCE	RESOURCES/NOTES
Edmond Ogden can be found in Pinckney's *Reminiscenes of Catskill* as part of a document dated August 23, 1793, "for the purpose of raising the sum of Four hundred pounds, to have an academy erected at the Landing, in said town of Catskill." Edmond was listed as a contributor of two shares. At the time of the contribution, Henry was seven years old. Two years later, Edmond contributed again. Beyond 1799, there is no evidence that Edmond lived in Catskill or anywhere. Sybil is mentioned as a tavern owner in Beers: "The following were innkeepers in this town [Catskill] in 1803: Sibel Ogden…"	Pinckney, *Reminiscences of Catskill*. Beers, *History of Greene County*, "Education-Innkeeper," 121.	
There are no records of any legal transactions in Catskill that would indicate that Edmond had been a lawyer.	Smith, *Daily Mail*.	Catskill Public Library.

Fact	Source	Resources/Notes
Henry Hill refers to Sybil's tavern on p. 19 in his *Recollections* when he writes about Catskill: "The Masonic brethren in their parades and marching made an imposing appearance. The lodge met in the chamber of Mrs. Ogden's tavern." He mentions her again on p. 21: "In or near the lower part of Main Street, were Judge Day, Lyman Hall, Joseph Graham and Tertullus Luddington, with their stores [Tertullus was Sybil's younger brother], the Widow Ogden and her tavern."	Hill, *Recollections of an Octogenarian*, 21.	Catskill Public Library.
Sybil was widowed when Edmond died of yellow fever at forty-four. Sybil was thirty-eight, and Henry was thirteen. By the time Henry was thirteen, Sybil was in business for herself. Six years later, she sold the business for almost four times what she had paid for it, and her son was ready to be on his own. In the Ogden-Webster deed of 1803, Sybil is listed as "widow."	Grantee Index M–R, 1800, *Index of Deeds*. Greene County, NY. 1804, Sybil Ogden/Reuben Webster. 1810, Sybil Ogden and Henry Ogden/Lyman Hall Pension File #7777, "Ogden, Edmond; Sebal."	Greene County Clerk's Office on the first floor of the courthouse in Catskill.
Catskill had an epidemic of yellow fever during 1803, when Sybil purchased her tavern. Her husband's case of yellow fever was three years prior to the epidemic.	Mitchill and Miller, "Remarks on the Yellow Fever." Smith, "1803 Yellow Fever."	Articles on yellow fever by Mabel Parker Smith provided by her daughter, Barbara S. Rivette.

FACT	SOURCE	RESOURCES/NOTES
Mabel Parker Smith stated that Sybil's tavern on Main and Greene Streets in Catskill was known as Ogden's Corner. The property the tavern was on is well documented in land transaction records. Sybil paid $732 for the property and sold it for $2,750 only six years later.	Smith, *Daily Mail*, January 11, 1978.	Articles by Mabel Parker Smith provided by her daughter, Barbara S. Rivette.
Sybil was listed in a land transaction with her son, Henry, on August 1, 1810, for $237.20 with John and Gitty DuBois for lots 13 and 14, lying on the east side of Water Street and northwest side of Greene Street leading from "Ogden's corner westerly to the creek and bounded…"	1803, Sybil Ogden/Stephen Bayard. 1810, John DuBois and Gitty DuBois/Sybil Ogden and Henry Ogden. 1806, Sybil Ogden/Joseph Graham.	County clerk's office, Catskill, NY.
Henry Ogden of Catskill married Julia Peck of Unadilla in 1810 in the Old Church of Catskill.	File in Vedder Memorial Research Library. Information was recorded on an index card in a box marked "church records." A verification of this was sent to me in letter form by Shirley McGrath of the Vedder Research Center.	Memorial Library and Research Center, RD 1, Coxsackie, NY.
Sybil's son, Henry Ogden, was born in Dutchess County, became a prominent lawyer in Catskill and later moved to Unadilla. He was a member of the state assembly in 1820, 43rd session. He reared a family of four sons and two daughters. His grave and the graves of his wife and four of his children are in a family plot in Unadilla.	*History of Otsego County.*	New York State Historical Association Library, Cooperstown, NY, and the Putnam County historian's office.
Two sons, Richard and Fredrick, are buried in California.	File on Richard Ogden in Washington, D.C.	National Archives, Washington, D.C.

FACT	SOURCE	RESOURCES/NOTES
It is likely that Sybil took her son, her daughter-in-law, her infant grandson and her $2,750 up the Catskill Turnpike to Unadilla to start a new life that continued for thirty years. Her son was active in law and politics.	Letter from Julia in the pension files. U.S. military records file, Washington, D.C.	U.S. Military Records files in Washington Archives Center.
Henry Ogden was as active a participant in his community as his grandfather Colonel Ludington had been.		Town historian and village historian, Unadilla, NY.
Henry served on the vestry of St. Matthew's Church almost to the time of his death.	Noble, "Records of St. Matthew's Church."	
Henry was an officer of the Unadilla Masons, Freedom Lodge No. 179.	"The Beginnings of Masonry in Otsego County, N.Y." American Lodge of Research Transactions 4, 1946–47.	The Chancellor Robert R. Livingston Masonic Library of Grand Lodge, 71 West 23rd Street, NY.
In 1817, Henry was a member of the Susquehanna Bridge Company, created for the purpose of building a bridge across the Susquehanna River. He was elected to the New York Assembly in 1820. He was elected as one of Unadilla's first village trustees in 1828 with Isaac Hayes, Boswell Wright, Daniel Cone and Johnson Wright.	Hunt, *Village Beautiful*.	Unadilla Public Library.
He was a participant in the "Unadilla Hunt," also called the "Oxford Chase." This group was known for its hunting expeditions and lavish parties.	*History of Otsego County.*	Otsego County libraries.
Julia was a member of the Female Missionary Association of St. Matthew's Church, as was her daughter Emily. Mary Ogden died at fifteen, too young to have been in the association.	Watson, "Records of the Female Missionary Association."	

FACT	SOURCE	RESOURCES/NOTES
There are no known school records, church records or community service records for Sybil's grandsons, Richard, Frederick and Edmund.	There are no sources available.	
Edmund Augustus Ogden was born to Henry and Julia on February 20, 1811.	See USMA files and handwritten letter from Henry stating Edmund's birth date.	USMA Library/Special Collections at West Point.
Edmund Augustus Ogden was a brevet major and assistant quartermaster, United States Army. He died with distinction at Fort Riley, Kansas, on August 3, 1855, at forty-four. His widow is listed as Eliza Loomis. They were married in 1835. The couple had eight children.	Ancestry.com. Cullum, *Biographical Register.* Index to Old Wars Pension Files 1815–1826, Vol. 2, L-2, trans. by V.D. White, 822. *New York Observer*, October 18, 1855. *Kansas Territorial Register*, "For Fort Riley," July 21, 1855. James D. Pinckney, "Cholera at Fort Riley," *Kansas Weekly Herald: Leavenworth Section*, August 11, 1855. Omer, "Army Hospital."	
Additional information on Sybil's grandchildren can be found in family correspondence available at the New-York Historical Society Library.	"Ludington Family Papers," MS 2962, New-York Historical Society's Research Library. Collection donated by Jane Ludington in 2015.	New-York Historical Society Library.

FACT	SOURCE	RESOURCES/NOTES
St. Matthew's Cemetery behind the Presbyterian church is the resting place of Henry, his wife and four of his children. Henry Ogden, Esq., died on November 27, 1837; Emily, died October 9, 1841, 21 yrs. old, buried in Unadilla, July 26, 1849, brought from Maryland; Julia, wife of Henry Esq., died November 22, 1849, 58 yrs. old, buried January 3, 1850; Mary, buried August 21, 1833; Henry A., buried December 11, 1854; Edmund Augustus, Major U.S. Army, born Catskill, NY, February 20, 1811, died Fort Riley, Kansas, August 8, 1855. Richard and Frederick lived in California and are not buried with the family.	Deaths taken from the *Otsego Herald and Western Advertiser* and *Freeman's Journal*, Otsego County, New York newspaper, 1795–1840, Vol. 1, Gertrude A. Barber, 1932. Halsey, *Pioneers of Unadilla*.	
Sybil Ludington Ogden lived in Unadilla, NY, in February 1834. She was still living in Unadilla in 1838.	Pension record R7777.	U.S. Military Pension Records. Fold3.
Sybil's memory lives on in the Hudson River Valley.	See chapters 9 and 10 of this book.	

NOTES

Frontispiece

1. McMahon, "Sybil Ludington Has Her Day," A3. Sybil was the thirty-fifth woman to be honored on a U.S. postage stamp.

Introduction

2. Michals, "Sybil Ludington." "Ludington married in 1784, at 23, when she met *Edward* Ogden."
3. Sybil was born in 1761 and died in 1839 but never reached her seventy-eighth birthday.
4. See the back side of the U.S. postage stamp, which proclaims Sybil "rode her horse 'Star' alone through the Connecticut countryside."
5. See the back side of the DAR medal #20 printed in her honor: "Great Women of the American Revolution" and "Her mission was crucial to the patriot victory in Danbury."
6. At the time of her ride, Sybil was sixteen and no longer a child. Her mother was married at fourteen and was fifteen when she gave birth to Sybil. See NSCAR museum exhibit's reference to Sybil as "child patriot" in Washington, D.C.
7. Johnson, *Colonel Henry Ludington*, 45.
8. Ogden-Barker Deed, Dutchess County clerk's office, Liber 12, 62.
9. Pension File S 23152, Jonathan Carley, 1834, 18.
10. Pension File R7777, Conn. Navy, Ogden, Edmond; Sebal, 1839, 2.

11. Of interest here is that Lewis S. Patrick was the only historian I located who used the spelling of her name as it appears on her gravestone.
12. Lamb, *History of the City of New York*, 160.
13. Pelletreau, *History of Putnam County*, 692.
14. Conard, "Nelson Ludington," 480.
15. Patrick, "Secret Service of the American Revolution," 269.
16. Johnson, *Colonel Henry Ludington*, 90.
17. Also of interest is that the plaque at the base of her statue spells her name "Sybil," while the road marker a few feet away refers to her as "Sibyl." Another discrepancy is true at her burial site, with the road marker for her stone calling her "Sybil" and the gravestone calling her "Sibbell."
18. Ephlin, "Girl Who Outrode Paul Revere," 50–52.
19. Dacquino, "Little Research Goes a Long Way."
20. Dacquino, "New York Patriot."
21. *Best of New York Archives*, "New York Patriot."
22. Dacquino, *Sybil Ludington: Discovering the Life*.
23. Dacquino, *Hauntings of the Hudson River Valley*, cover.

Chapter 1

24. Pelletreau, *History of Putnam County*, 691. Pelletreau also mentions here that the Ludington house in Branford was destroyed by fire on May 20, 1754. Rebecca and Anne, the Colonel's younger sisters, perished in the fire.
25. Johnson, *Colonel Henry Ludington*, 35. (Pelletreau, on page 691 of his *History of Putnam County*, also calls Elisha "son of William 3d.")
26. Ibid., 35–36.
27. *Dutchess County Historical Society Year Book*, vol. 25, 1940, 80.
28. Patrick, "Secret Service of the American Revolution," 266. See also Johnson, *Colonel Henry Ludington*, 30–31.
29. Patrick, "Secret Service of the American Revolution," 267.
30. Ibid., 268.
31. Ibid.
32. *Dutchess County Historical Society Year Book*, vol. 30, 1945, 76.
33. Patrick, "Secret Service of the American Revolution," 274.
34. Ibid., 45.
35. *Dutchess County Historical Yearbook*, vol. 25, 1940, 81.
36. Patrick, "Secret Service of the American Revolution," 273.

37. Johnson, *Colonel Henry Ludington*, 39–40.
38. Patrick, "Secret Service of the American Revolution," 269.
39. Lamb, *History of the City of New York*, 212.
40. Ibid., footnote, 213.
41. Johnson, *Colonel Henry Ludington*, 214.
42. web.cortland.edu/woosterk/deming.html.

Chapter 2

43. Case, *Tryon's Raid*, 13.
44. Ibid., 16.
45. Diamant, *Revolutionary Women*, 67–68.
46. Bailey, *History of Danbury*, 68.
47. Ibid., 68–69.
48. Case, *Tryon's Raid*, 24.
49. Ibid.
50. Johnson, *Colonel Henry Ludington*, 219.
51. Wisconsin Society of the Sons of the American Revolution application for membership, National number 10483, State Number 158.
52. Patrick, "Secret Service of the American Revolution" (see sidebar on page 24).
53. Johnson, *Colonel Henry Ludington*, 89–91.
54. Rockwell, *History of Ridgefield*, 103–19.
55. Johnson, *Colonel Henry Ludington*, 89–91.
56. Case, *Tryon's Raid*, 43–44.
57. Ibid., 28.

Chapter 3

58. *Putnam County Courier*, "Revolutionary War Service of Local People."
59. *Congressional Record*, "Remarks of Hon. R. Barry."
60. Pelletreau, *History of Putnam County*, 692.
61. Beers, *Commemorative Biographical Record*, 978.
62. Johnson, *Colonel Henry Ludington*, 45.
63. Ibid., 219.

Chapter 4

64. Jacobus, *History and Genealogy*, vol. 2, part 2, 712.

65. Credit must be given here to Edward L. Woodyard of Armonk, New York, who conducted a genealogical search of the Ogden family, enabling me to search Connecticut records for Edmond Ogden.

66. Ogden children as listed in Jacobus, *History and Genealogy*, 713: "Ann born 11/2/1744, baptised 11/25—married 4/7/1762 to John Coley; Mary—born 4/3, baptised 4/26/1747—married 4/22/1770 to Nathan Sturges; Joseph born 3/1, baptised 3/19/1749—married 10/3/71 to Rachel Daniels; Humphrey—born 2/21, baptised 2/24/1751; Sarah—born 1/24, baptised 2/4/1753—married 12/24/72 to Stephen Hurlbut; Edmund [*sic*]—born 2/12, baptised 3/2/1755, died in New York State 9/16/99; married at Patterson, Putnam County, N.Y. 24, Oct. 1784 (pension rec.) to Sybil, who was living in 1838 in Unadilla, Otsego NY.; Eunice—born 12/28/56, baptised 1/16/57—married 11/19/78 to Pinkney Beers; Nathan—baptised 1/15/1759—married 4/13/1780 to Hannah Goodsell; Hannah—baptised at Weston 7/27/1760; Elizabeth—baptised 2/26/1763; Rhoda—baptised Aug. 3, 1766."

67. Jacobus, *History and Genealogy*, vol. 3, 239–40.

68. Ibid., 206.

69. Ibid., 206–7.

70. Ogden-Barker Deed, Dutchess County clerk's office, Liber 12, 62.

71. *Heads of Families at the First Census*, 81.

Chapter 5

72. Vedder, *Historic Catskill*, 68.

73. Pinckney, *Reminiscences of Catskill*, 77.

74. Hill, *Recollections of an Octogenarian*, 21.

75. Ogden-Barker Deed, Dutchess County clerk's office.

76. Mabel Parker Smith, a Greene County historian, wrote a series of four articles on Sybil Ludington Ogden in the *Catskill Daily Mail*, January 9–11, 1978.

77. Beers, *History of Greene County*, 142.

78. Mitchill and Miller, "Remarks on the Yellow Fever."

79. Beers, *History of Greene County*, 143.

80. Smith, "1803 Yellow Fever."

Chapter 6

81. *History of Otsego County*, 335.
82. *Unadilla Times*, "Historical Unadilla 1855–1930," 28.
83. Barber, *Death Notices*.
84. See Julia Ogden's letter in the Pension Application Files: "Edmond Ogden R7777."
85. Halsey, *Pioneers of Unadilla*, 142.
86. See application S 23152 for Jonathan Carley, 18.
87. Halsey, *Pioneers of Unadilla*, 173.
88. Goerlich, *At Rest in Unadilla*, 275.
89. *History of Otsego County*, 335.
90. See St. Matthew's Church records at the church rectory.
91. *History of Otsego County*, 26.
92. The Minutes of the Corporation from 1828, Village of Unadilla, located in Unadilla Town Hall.
93. Pelletreau, *History of Putnam County*, 615.
94. Johnson, *Colonel Henry Ludington*, 222.
95. Pride, *History of Fort Riley*, 87–90.

Chapter 7

96. Bell, "Sybil Ludington: Woman of Legend."
97. Bell, "Sybil Ludington: The Legend's Beginning."
98. Lamb, *History of the City of New York*, 160.
99. Bell, "Going Back to Sybil Ludington."
100. Ibid.
101. Johnson, *Colonel Henry Ludington*, viii.
102. Application file, W1911 James Mead.
103. Application file, David Mead S 9975.
104. Application file, W16987 Ezra Ferris.
105. Alexander McLeod application, S 11052.
106. Darley, *Call to Arms*.
107. Conard, "Nelson Ludington," vol. 17, 480.

Chapter 8

108. Hunt, "Sybil Ludington," 187–222, quote p. 187.
109. Paula Hunt, podcast, www.mitpressjournals.org/podcast/episode25_TNEQ.
110. Lamb, *History of the City of New York*, 159.
111. See Eschner, "Was There Really a Teenage, Female Paul Revere?"; Lewis, "Sybil Ludington: A Female Paul Revere?"
112. DAR, "DAR Museum Exhibition."
113. See ebay listing for DAR medal, www.ebay.com/itm/DAR-Medal-SYBIL-LUDINGTON-American-Revolutionary-War-/361229368164.
114. See NSCAR Museum, nscar.org/Documents/Features/Museum%20Powerpoint1617.pdf.
115. CAR website, nscar.org/NSCAR/AboutCAR/Headquarters.aspx.
116. Hunt, Sybil Ludington," 222.

Chapter 9

117. Stone, "Reenactment to Celebrate Sybil Ludington's Ride."
118. "Annual Sybil Ludington 50k and 25k," runsignup.com/Race/NY/Carmel/AnnualSybilLudington50kandTwoPersonRelay.
119. Nackman, "Sybil Rides Again."
120. See Town of Ridgefield, "Battle of Ridgefield Reenactment"; Ducey, "Hundreds Line Main Street."
121. Rodengen, *NRA: An American Legend*, 238.

Chapter 10

122. Letter in Jonathan Carley Deposition S23152, 9.
123. Lamb, *History of the City of New York*, vi.

BIBLIOGRAPHY

Abbot, E.F. *Sybil Ludington: Revolutionary War Rider*. New York: Feiwel and Friends, 2016.

Amstel, Marsha. *Sybil Ludington's Midnight Ride*. Minneapolis, MN: Carol Rhoda Books, 2000.

Bailey, James Montgomery. Comp. with additions by Susan Benedict Hill. *History of Danbury, Conn., 1684–1896*. New York: Burr Printing House, 1896.

Baily, F.E. *Early Connecticut Marriages*. Baltimore: Genealogical Publishing Co., 1968.

Barber, Gertrude A. *Death Notices Taken from the* Otsego Herald *and* Western Advertiser *and* Freemans Journal. Otsego County, New York Newspapers. Vol. 1, 1932.

Baumhart, Carl M. "The Teenager Who Outrode Paul Revere." *New York Herald Tribune*, July 17, 1960.

Beers, J.B., ed. *History of Greene County*. New York: J.B. Beers and Co., 1884.

Beers, J.H. *Commemorative Biographical Record: Dutchess and Putnam Counties*. New York: J.B. Beers and Co., 1897.

Bell, J.L. "Going Back to Sybil Ludington." Boston 1775/blogspot.com, January 14, 2012.

———. "Sybil Ludington: The Legend's Beginning." Boston 1775/blogspot.com, November 30, 2006.

———. "Sybil Ludington: Woman of Legend." Boston 1775/blogspot.com, January 1, 2006.

Berkin, Carol. *Revolutionary Mothers: Women in the Struggle for American Independence*. New York: Alfred A. Knopf, 2005.

Bernstein, Paula. "A Legendary Woman Rides onto a Stamp." *Daily News*, March 20, 1975.

Berry, Erick. *Sybil Ludington's Ride*. New York: Viking Press, 1952.

Best of New York Archives: Selections from the Magazine, 2001–2011. N.Y. State Partnership Trust, 2017.

Blake, William J. *The History of Putnam County, N.Y.* New York: Baker & Scribner, 1849.

Bowie, Jocelyn. "Putnam Will Give This Lady a Lift." *Reporter Dispatch* (White Plains, NY), January 29, 1985.

Bowman, Fred Q. *8,000 More Vital Records of Eastern N.Y. State*. Rhinebeck, NY: Kinship, 1991.

Braley, Berton. "Sybil Ludington's Ride." *Sunday Star: This Week Magazine* (Washington, D.C.), April 14, 1940.

Brown, Drollene P. *Sybil Rides for Independence*. Niles, IL: Albert Whitman and Company, 1985.

Brutting, Margaret, et. al., eds. "An Historic Biographical Profile of the Town of Kent, Putnam County, N.Y." Town of Kent: New York Bicentennial Commission, 1976.

Carboni, Bob. *General William Tryon's Raid*. Wilton, CT: Wilton Historical Society Library, 1963.

Case, James R. *Tryon's Raid*. Danbury, CR: privately printed, 1927.

Clyne, Patricia Edwards. *Patriots in Petticoats*. New York: Dodd, Mead & Co., 1976.

Cobbs, Phyllis. "Putnam's Pride: Sybil Ludington and Enoch Crosby." *Patent Trader*, Bicentennial Edition, February 1, 1975.

Collaborative History of Putnam County, N.Y. Produced by the Putnam County Government, 2012.

Conard, Howard Louis. *Encyclopedia of the History of Missouri: A Compendium of History and Biography for Ready Reference*. New York: Southern History Company, 1901.

———. "Nelson Ludington, Lumberman and Banker." *National Magazine* 17, November 1892–April 1893.

Congressional Record. Appendix A3168. "Remarks of Hon. R. Barry, of New York at Garden Party, National Woman's Party—Extension of Remarks of Hon. Barry of New York in House of Representatives, Monday, May 20, 1963."

Cullum, George W. *Biographical Register of the Officers and Graduates of the U.S. Military Academy of West Point*. Vol. 1, nos. 1 to 1000. Boston: Houghton Mifflin, 1891.

Dacquino, Vincent T. *Hauntings of the Hudson River Valley: An Investigative Journey*. Charleston, SC: The History Press, 2007.

———. "A Little Research Goes A Long Way." *Read Magazine* 54, no. 14 (March 11, 2005).

———. "New York Patriot." *New York Archives* 6, no. 4 (Spring 2007).

———. *Sybil Ludington: Discovering the Life of a Revolutionary War Hero*. Fleischmanns, NY: Purple Mountain Press, 2007.

———. *Sybil Ludington Ogden: Grandmother's Story*. Fleischmanns, NY: Purple Mountain Press, 2012.

Danbury News Times. "Huntington Statue Ready for Library Ceremonies." September 9, 1971.

DAR. "DAR Museum Exhibition Explores Early American Myths." October 6, 2006. www.dar.org/national-society/media-center/news-releases/dar-museum-exhibition-explores-early-american-myths.

Darley, Stephen. *Call to Arms: The Patriot Militia in the 1777 British Raid on Danbury, Connecticut*. N.p., 2015.

Diamant, Lincoln, ed. *Revolutionary Women in the War for American Independence: A One-Volume Revised Edition of Elizabeth Ellet's 1848 Landmark Series*. Westport, CT: Praeger, 1998.

Ducey, Kerry Anne. "Hundreds Line Main Street for Battle of Ridgefield Reenactment." Hamlet Hub, April 29, 2017. news.hamlethub.com/ridgefield/life/55981-hundreds-line-main-street-for-battle-of-ridgefield-reenactment.

Dutchess County Historical Society Yearbook. Poughkeepsie, NY: Dutchess County Historical Society vol. 25, 1940, and vol. 30, 1945.

Engle, Paul. *Women in the Revolution*. Chicago: Follett Publishing Co., 1976.

Ephlin, Donald L. "The Girl Who Outrode Paul Revere." *Coronet*, November 1949.

Eschner, Kate. "Was There Really a Teenage, Female Paul Revere?" Smithsonian.com, April 26, 2017. www.smithsonianmag.com/smithsonianmag/was-there-really-teenage-female-paul-revere-180962993.

Foley, Janet Wethy. *Early Settlers of New York State: Their Ancestors and Descendants*. Baltimore: Genealogical Publishing Co., 1993. Originally published serially. Vol. 1, 1934; Vol. 9, 1942. Reprinted in two volumes.

Frost, Rev. Jim. "A Chronological History of the Presbyterian Church of Patterson-Pawling, N.Y." Patterson, NY: Presbyterian Society, 1993.

Gallt, J.A. *Dear Old Greene County*. Catskill, NY: privately printed by the author, 1915.

Geller, Herb. *A Fight for Liberty*. Bridgeport, CT: Post Publishing Co., 1976.

———. "Miss Ludington: Putnam Girl Paul Revere Influenced the Battle of 1777." *Patent Trader* 45, no. 10, June 9, 1957.

———. "Sixteen-Year-Old Girl Rouses Militia to Fight British." *Patent Trader*, May 21, 1959.

Goerlich, Shirley B. *At Rest in Unadilla*. Sidney, NY: RSG Publishing, 1987.

Grant, Anne. *Danbury's Burning*. New York: Henry Z. Walck, 1976.

Green, Margaret Ludington. *Samuel Ludington: Ancestors and Descendants*. Smyrna, TN: published by the author, 1968.

Greenbie, Marjorie B. "The Ride of Sybil Ludington." Washington, D.C.: Congressional Record, Appendix A3169, May 20, 1963.

Gross, Eric. "Sybil Statue Cured of Mouth Foam." *Putnam Courier-Trader*, June 14, 1989.

Hall, Marjory. *See the Red Sky*. Philadelphia: Westminster Press, 1963.

Halsey, Frances Whiting. *The Old New York Frontier, 1614–1800*. New York: Charles Scribner's Sons, 1917.

———. *The Pioneers of Unadilla Village, 1784–1840*. Unadilla, NY: St. Matthew's Church, 1902.

Hasbrouck, Frank, ed. *The History of Dutchess County, New York*. Poughkeepsie, NY: S.A. Matthieu, 1909.

Haviland, J.C. "The Unsung Ride of Sybil Ludington." *North County News*, *This Week Magazine* supplement, April 24, 1985.

Heads of Families at First Census of the United States of America Taken in the Year 1790. New York Heritage Series. Number I. Washington, D.C.: Government Printing Office, 1908.

Hill, Henry. *Recollections of an Octogenarian*. Boston: Lothrop and Co., 1884.

History of Otsego County. Philadelphia: Everts and Ferris, Press of J.B. Lippincott & Co., 1878.

Hollister, Gideon Hiram. *History of Connecticut*. Vol. 2. New Haven, CT: Durrie and Peck, 1855.

Hominick, Judy, and Jeanne Spreier. *Ride for Freedom: The Story of Sybil Ludington*. New York: Silver Moon Press, 2001.

Horne, Field. *The Greene County Catskills: A History*. Hensonville, NY: Black Dome Press Corp., 1994.

Howard, Jan. "Uncovering the Remarkable Story of Sybil Ludington." *Newtown Bee*, April 11, 2001.

Hunt, Paula D. "Sybil Ludington, the Female Paul Revere: The Making of a Revolutionary War Heroine." *New England Quarterly* 88, no. 2 (June 2015).

Hunt, Walter L. *The Village Beautiful*. Unadilla, NY, 1957.

Jacobus, Donald Lines. *History and Genealogy of the Families of Old Fairfield*. Vol. 1; Vol. 2, Part 1; Vol. 2, Part 2; Vol. 3. N.p., 1932.

Jewell, Willitt C. *Putnam County in Southern New York*. New York: Lewis Historical Publishing Company, 1946.

Johnson, Willis Fletcher. *Colonel Henry Ludington: A Memoir*. New York: published by his grandchildren, Lavinia Elizabeth and Charles Henry Ludington, 1907.

Jones, Keith Marshall, III. *Farmers Against the Crown: A Comprehensive Account of the Revolutionary War Battle in Ridgefield, Connecticut, April 27, 1777*. Ridgefield: Connecticut Publishing Company, 2002.

Jones, Thomas. *History of New York During the Revolutionary War*. New York: New-York Historical Society, 1879. Reprinted by Arno Press, 1968.

Kansas Historical Register. "To Maj. A.E. Ogden for Favors from Fort Riley." August 4, 1855.

Khasru, B.Z. 'Famous Americans Meet at Fair." *Reporter Dispatch*, April 2, 1993.

———. "Florida Woman Traces Her Roots to Putnam County War Heroine." *Reporter Dispatch*, February 25, 1995.

Kruk, Jonathan. "Sybil's Ride: A Fictional/Historic Account." *Nimham Times Magazine*, March 1998.

Lamb, Martha Joanna. *History of the City of New York: Its Origin and Rise and Progress*. Vol. 2. N.p.: A.S. Barnes & Co., 1880.

Landon, Bren. "DAR Museum Exhibition Explores Early American Myths." Dar.org, October 6, 2006. www.dar.org/national-society/media-center/news-releases/dar-museum-exhibition-explores-early-american-myths.

Leroux, Marilyn. "Historic Ride across Putnam Set to Music." *Reporter Dispatch*, April 3, 1993.

Lewis, Jone Johnson. "Sybil Ludington: A Female Paul Revere?" ThoughtCo, July 31, 2017. womenshistory.about.com/od/waramrevolution/p/ludington_ride.htm.

Ludington, Ethel Saltus, and Louis Effinghamde Forest, ed. *Ludington-Saltus Records*. N.p., 1925.

"The Ludington Family Papers." MS 2962. New-York Historical Society's Research Library. Collection donated by Jane Ludington in 2015.

MacCracken, Henry Noble. *Old Dutchess Forever!* New York: Hastings House, 1956.

Mahoney, Tom. "Night Riders of the American Revolution." *American Legion Magazine*, June 1972.

Masonic History of Unadilla, N.Y. Unadilla, NY: Press of the Times, 1902.

Masters, Ann V. "Anna Hyatt Huntington Carves Female Paul Revere." *Bridgeport Sunday Post*, August 21, 1960.

McDevitt, Robert F. *Connecticut Attacked: A British Viewpoint, Tryon's Raid on Danbury*. Chester, CT: Pequot Press, 1974.

McLaughlin, Tami. "Restaurant Salutes Sybil's Historic Run." *Patent Trader*, September 21, 1983.

McMahon, Jane. "Sybil Ludington Has Her Day." *Reporter Dispatch*, March 26, 1975.

McNamara, Tom. "U.S. Stamp to Honor Sybil Ludington." *Reporter Dispatch*, December 30,1974.

Merkling, Frank. "Sybil Rides Again: Hear Her Story." *News-Times Sunday Magazine*, March 21, 1993.

Michals, Debra. "Sybil Ludington." National Women's History Museum, 2017. www.womenshistory.org/education-resources/biographies/sybil-ludington.

The Midnight Ride of Sybil Ludington and the Mystery of the Statue of King George III and His Horse. Wilton, CT: Pimpewaug Press, 1976.

Miller, Helen Coats. "A Portrait of Old Dutchess." *National Historic Magazine* 77, 1943.

The Minutes of the Corporation from 1828. Village of Unadilla, NY, Unadilla Town Hall.

Mitchill, Samuel Latham, MD, and Edward Miller, MD. "Remarks on the Yellow Fever at Catskill, 1803." *Medical Repository and Review of American Publications on Medicine, Surgery, and the Auxiliary Branches of Science*, Second Hexade, II, 1805.

Moore, James M. "The Night of the Fire." *Yankee*, April 1970.

Muscarella, Richard. "Sybil's Putnam Ride Alerted Troops in American Revolution." *Putnam Courier-Trader*, May 18, 1995.

Nackman, Barbara Livingston. "Sybil Rides Again." *Journal News*, April 29, 2007.

Noble, Curtis. "The Records of St. Matthew's Church." Unadilla, NY, 1850.

NSCAR Museum. "Freedom's Thunder 2016–2017 Exhibit." nscar.org/Documents/Features/Museum%20Powerpoint1617.pdf.

Ogden-Barker Deed, Dutchess County clerk's office. Liber 12.

Omer, George E. "An Army Hospital: From Dragoons to Rough Riders—Fort Riley, 1853–1903." *Kansas Historical Quarterly* 33, no. 4 (Winter 1957).

Patent Trader. "NOW Remembers Sybil, Putnam's Paul Revere." December 17, 1972.

———. "Sibyl Ludington's Ride Immortalized in Bronze." February 22, 1959.

———. "Stamp Covers Offered." February 15, 1975.

Patrick, Lewis S. *The Ludington Family: The First Name in America.* Marinette, WI: Independent Press, 1886.

Patrick, Louis S. "Secret Service of the American Revolution." *Connecticut Magazine* 11, no. 2, 1907.

Pearlman, Skip. "Ludington Memorial Race Set." *Reporter Dispatch,* February 23, 1982.

Pelletreau, William S. *History of Putnam County, New York.* Philadelphia: W.W. Preston, 1886. Reprint, Brewster, NY: Landmarks Preservation Committee of Southeast Museum, 1975. Reprint, Interlaken, NY: Heart of the Lakes, 1988.

Pelton, Robert W. "The Midnight Ride of Sibyl Ludington." *New York Alive* 9, no. 2 (March/April 1989).

Pension Application Files. "Edmond Ogden R7777." U.S. War Department. September 8, 1838.

Pinckney, James D. *Reminiscences of Catskill: Local Sketches.* Catskill, NY: J.B. Hall, 1868.

Pollack, Michael. "Heroine of 1777 Still All in a Revolutionary Lather." *New York Times,* October 22, 1995.

Pride, W.F. *The History of Fort Riley.* N.p., 1926.

Putnam County Courier (Carmel, NY). "Five Historic Roadside Markers Dedicated by DAR Monday." May 17, 1935.

———. "History Repeats Itself?" March 1965.

———. "Revolutionary War Service of Local People Cited at the Dedication of Road Markers." September 14, 1934.

Record of Service of Connecticut Men in the War of the Revolution (Compiled by Authority of the General Assembly, Hartford). Hartford, CT, 1889.

Reporter Dispatch. "Living History Fair." April 2, 1993.

———. "Spirit of 76." March 25, 1975.

Roberts, James A. *New York in the Revolution as Colony and State.* Albany, NY: Press of Brandow Printing Co., 1898.

Rockwell, George L. *History of Ridgefield, Connecticut.* Ridgefield, CT, published by the author, 1927.

Rodengen, Jeffrey L. *NRA: An American Legend.* N.p.: Write Stuff Enterprises, 2002.

Ross, Emily. "The Female Paul Revere." *Daughters of the American Revolution Magazine*, April 1967.

Sheperd, James. *William Ludington of Malden, Mass, and East Haven, Conn., and His Descendents*. Boston: Press of David Clopp and Son, 1904. Reprinted from the *New England Historical and Genealogical Register*, January 1904.

Siegel, Suzie. "Teenage Rider Finally Revered." *Tribune* (Tampa, FL), January 30, 1995.

Smith, Mabel Parker. "1803 Yellow Fever Made Catskill Famous: Treatment Strenuous but Some Survived." *Daily Mail* (Catskill, NY), part 1, September 8, 1981.

———. "Unsung Heroine of Revolution Became Inn-Keeper on Busy Main Street Corner in Early Catskill." *Daily Mail* (Catskill, NY), article in four parts, January 9–12,1978.

Stephenson, Isaac. *Recollections of a Long Life, 1829–915.*Chicago: printed privately, 1915.

Stone, Adam. "Reenactment to Celebrate Sybil Ludington Ride." Examinernews.com, April 25, 2012. www.theexaminernews.com/ reenactment-to-celebrate-sybils-ride.

Sunday New Yorker. "A Tree Grows in Stormville." January 27, 1952.

Sybil of the American Revolution. New York: Abigail Adams Smith Museum (playbill), April 1 and 4, 1993.

Thomas, Richard. "Sybil Ludington, Heroine: Who's Who on U.S. Stamps?" *Linns Stamp News*, May 8, 1989.

Torrey, Raymond H. "Signs to Mark Historic Ride of Revolutionary Heroine." *New York Herald Tribune*, September 17, 1934.

Tower, Samuel. "Contributions to the Cause Stamps." *New York Times*, March 16, 1975.

Town of Ridgefield. "Battle of Ridgefield Reenactment (Announcement)." Ridgefield.org, April 29, 2017. www.ridgefieldct.org/economic-community-development-commission/events/2533.

Townsend, Louise P. "Sybil Ludington: Revolutionary War Heroine." Enoch Crosby Chapter of the Daughters of the American Revolution. Dedication ceremony speech, June 3, 1961.

Unadilla Times: A Supplement, vol. 76, no. 7. "Historical Unadilla 1855–1930: 75th Anniversary Ed." June 6, 1930.

Vedder, J.V.V. *Historic Catskill*. N.p., 1922.

———. *History of Greene County, 1651–1800*. Catskill, NY: County Historian, 1927.